By
ONES
By
&TWOS

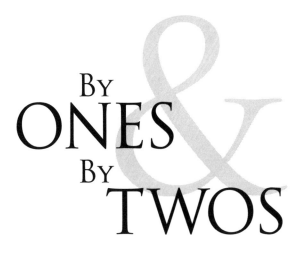

By ONES & By TWOS

BUILDING SUCCESSFUL RELATIONSHIPS
BETWEEN
MARRIEDS AND SINGLES IN MINISTRY

JEANNIE LOCKERBIE STEPHENSON

Association of Baptists for World Evangelism
P.O. Box 8585
Harrisburg, PA 17105–8585
(717) 774–7000
abwe@abwe.org

ABWE Canada
980 Adelaide St. South, Suite 34
London, Ontario N6E 1R3
(519) 690–1009
office@abwecanada.org

 PUBLISHING®

BY ONES & BY TWOS
Building Successful Relationships Between Marrieds and Singles in Ministry

First printing, 1983 William Carey Library, Pasadena, California 91104
Second printing, 1985 William Carey Library, Pasadena, California 91104
Revised edition copyright renewed © 2008 ABWE Publishing, Harrisburg, Pennsylvania 17105

Library of Congress Cataloging-in-Publication Data
(application pending)

Stephenson, Jeannie Lockerbie

By Ones & By Twos
    Missionaries—Psychology, Interpersonal relations
    ISBN: 978-1-888796-42-1

Printed in the United States of America

DEDICATION

To my SINGLE friends:
BECKY DAVEY, with whom I started my missionary career, and LYNN SILVERNALE, with whom I shared a home for more than 25 years,

and

To my MARRIED friends:
MARILOU LONG and ELEANOR WALSH who, with their husbands, Jim and Jay, exemplify godly marriages.

ACKNOWLEDGMENTS

To those who made this book become a reality:

Shirley Brinkerhoff, who felt the book should be updated and reprinted and passed that challenge on to me. Then in spite of health and other challenges, she provided guidelines and suggestions throughout the project.

Kristen Stagg, my colleague in ABWE Publications and the voice in my head that makes me look for better ways of saying things.

Carol Bibighaus, who after years of service in Hong Kong, now serves as director of Singles Ministry, guiding and encouraging ABWE's single men and women. Her insights and sharpness in correcting errors helped in producing this book.

A young woman (for security reasons she must remain anonymous) who wrote large blocks of material in areas where I had no experience and critiqued what I had written.

And to **my husband, Wally,** who helped and encouraged me in so many ways.

THANK YOU

TABLE OF CONTENTS

Jeannie: For more than thirty years I served as a missionary nurse, a teacher for missionary children, and primarily as the founder and director of a publishing and distributing house called the Literature Division. By God's grace this became the world's largest producer of Christian literature in the Bengali language and is now largely in the hands of capable Bangladeshi men and women. My place of service was in Chittagong, East Pakistan, as it was known until 1971 when the nation of Bangladesh was born.

During those years I saw the need for clearer communication and overall better interpersonal relationships between the married and non-married members of the missionary team. This need is no less critical in non-missionary circles.

I have spoken frequently on this subject at Bible colleges and at the candidate classes of my mission agency, ABWE (Association of Baptists for World Evangelism), with offices in Harrisburg, Pennsylvania, and London, Ontario.

When I wrote the first two editions of this book, I was single. That changed on August 24, 1996. I've asked Wally Stephenson, my husband, to explain:

Wally: I met Jeannie for the first time in 1995. The meeting had been arranged as a result of my writing fifty-three articles telling of God's gracious help following the deaths of my wife, Louise, and my daughter, Ruth, in a car accident on May 22, 1993. Wendell

Kempton, who was then president of ABWE, gave my fledgling work to Jeannie and told her, "Meet this man and get his manuscript published."

Because of the experiences I had been through, Jeannie expected to meet a sad, short, shriveled-up old man. Instead, a tall man with a big smile bounced out of the church where we met and said, "Let's go to Red Lobster for lunch." Sitting across from her, it did not take me two minutes to recognize I was in the presence of a classy Christian lady. I mused, *Too bad our ministries are so different and 9,000 miles apart.* After serving for twenty-nine years as a church planter and pastor in Ontario, Louise and I had gone to South Africa for what we expected would be a church-planting ministry that lasted for many years to come. Following thirty-three years of missionary service in Bangladesh, ABWE asked Jeannie to move to Harrisburg, Pennsylvania, to be the director of Publications. This included producing the *Message* magazine and books telling what God is doing in the world today.

After our lunch at Red Lobster the hammer fell. Jeannie told me I had written excellent, practical material, but it had to be totally rewritten in a different style. I swallowed my pride and agreed. I rewrote furiously between other commitments during an eight-week speaking tour in Atlantic Canada.

During ABWE's annual conference in July 1995, Jeannie and I spent as much time as we could editing the manuscript. But there was much work still to do, and I had a ticket to return to Durban, South Africa. Then the South African Consulate came to the rescue! Totally out of character, the consulate in Toronto lost my application, and I had to start again. Unexpectedly, I had some time on my hands. What would I do?

I arranged to fly to the ABWE Headquarters in Harrisburg. For four intensely busy days Jeannie and I wrote and rewrote, laughed and cried, prayed and went out to eat together. With all her questions and our discussions, Jeannie came to know me well.

We planned how we would stay in touch regarding last-minute changes, adjustments, and negotiations with publishers. Two days later I was in the air to Durban.

I didn't see Jeannie again until April 1996. But I phoned every Wednesday to discuss revisions in the manuscript and the progress toward publication. Each phone call ended with talk of personal things like the weather, what each was doing, and the price of tea in China. It was delightful to talk to her. I was always so happy afterwards and so was the telephone company, which was collecting $2 a minute.

In January 1996, Jeannie was back in Bangladesh and India. One day I thought I would like to talk to her as a nice surprise. I phoned the number on her itinerary, which I assumed was the family with whom she was staying in Kolkata, India. Instead it was a business. I tried and tried to make the uninterested man on the opposite end of the line understand that I wanted to speak to a certain family, with whom Jeannie was supposed to be staying. I learned that the family lived next door and he would send someone to bring them to the phone. A woman finally came and told me that Jeannie was not there. The speaker had no idea where she was. "Okay," I said, "I'll phone back in two days." I did. Same story. I was in a stew. Then a little voice inside me said, *Wally, if Jeannie is just a casual friend, why do you care so much?*

The fact of our separate ministries was a gigantic barrier to me. That wall was broken down when President Kempton and I met in Harrisburg to discuss a new ministry. I was appointed director of Compassionate Ministries, helping people who were struggling with grief and loss following any number of circumstances.

After that, Ma Bell's phone lines heated up. Our courting would not make a Harlequin romance, but we got the job done. And the book we'd been working on, *Through Tears to Triumph*, was also published. Jeannie and I were engaged in Toronto on May 26 and married in Harrisburg on August 24, 1996.

We have combined our ministries to complement each other. In churches and colleges from Florida to British Columbia and from California to Nova Scotia, we have spoken together about missions and given presentations called "Challenging Children to Serve the Lord" and "Helping Hurting People." We have also spoken and taught in Bible colleges in South Africa, Ghana, Togo, Kenya, England, Ireland, Trinidad, Jamaica, India, Bangladesh, Nepal, the Philippines, Thailand, and Mongolia.

Jeannie and I have discussed the numerous, incredible twists and turns that had to happen to put us together. There is only one explanation: God. He is so good!

Jeannie: While I will be the primary author, Wally Stephenson will be prominent in this edition of the book. From time to time, his words about his insights and experiences will appear, and he will be identified as the writer.

—Jeannie Lockerbie Stephenson
London, Ontario, 2008

CHAPTER 1

What's the Problem?

Wimbledon: The very name of this tennis venue rings with excitement and drama!

As opponents face each other across the net, one thought is uppermost in their minds: to play well and win.

Sometimes the game is a singles match. Tennis, however, is often played by doubles: two partners competing with another two players. But singles or doubles, the court, the equipment, and the rules are the same. The goal for each opponent is to win the prize.

The tennis analogy applies to the game of life and to Christian service also. We would do well to remember the unified purpose and not become caught up with the status of the "players," dividing them into two categories: the married couples and the singles.

BECOMING A SINGLE MISSIONARY

I had never run into the term "single missionary" until I became one. In the business and professional world a person is an executive, a teacher, or a nurse, not a "single" executive, teacher, or nurse. I was introduced to the term in missionary candidate seminar the year I joined ABWE.

During my candidate training, each member had a work assignment. Mine was in an area where a large carton blocked the ping-pong table. Everyone wanted that section cleared first, but I could not lift the heavy box. Going to the stairway, I called to the first person I saw, a young married man, and asked, "Would you help me, please?"

I still remember his answer: "I might have known. I was warned that I would be helping the 'single girls' all the time. It's already started."

My marital status had nothing to do with the fact that I had sought his help. Had I had five husbands, I still could not have lifted that heavy box!

Even the word "single" can pose problems. I once received what I took to be a great compliment: "She has done more in this area than any other single person." Wow! I thought that meant that I had accomplished more in the particular area than anybody else! Later I learned that the speaker meant more than any other unmarried person. Since I knew that no other unmarried person had tackled that particular project, the compliment fizzled.

When I started raising funds for missionary service, I was told how difficult it would be because I was single. That was not so. Following fifteen months of speaking in churches, homes, and colleges, my colleague Becky Davey and I boarded the SS *Bintang* for a thirty-day sea voyage. Becky and I did not just raise money; we found a support team, many of whom continue their finances and prayer support to this day.

A few years after I settled in Bangladesh, I invited a newly arrived, married missionary over to my house. We chatted and laughed and had fun as we drank our coffee. We talked about where we lived in North America, shared our travel experiences, and spoke about the house she and her family would soon move into. As she was leaving, she remarked, "I never expected I'd be able to sit and talk like this with a single girl."

I recall wondering, *Why would she suppose she wouldn't be able to talk with me?* At the same time I felt good about the rapport we had established. She continues to be a good friend.

What is more conducive to ongoing effective Christian service than rapport and harmony among fellow workers? What is more destructive than poor interpersonal relationships?

One area where harmony can become discord is in the relationship between unmarried workers and their married co-workers. In the missionary world this deserves special consideration because statistics show that seventy-six percent of the overseas missionary force is married. This leaves a sizable twenty-four percent of the total missionary force who, by choice or circumstance, are not married, the vast majority of whom are women.

Yet, who is to say whether today's single missionary will be one of tomorrow's marrieds, or if today's married missionary will be tomorrow's widow or widower?

Wally — Single Again : On May 21, 1960, I married Louise Hyde. We were partners in planting and working in churches, both in Canada and in South Africa.

On May 22, 1993, Louise and our daughter Ruth were killed in a car accident. After the accident it took me a while to grasp the scary reality that I was single. This was new territory. I was most uncomfortable, and it probably showed.

Three months after the accident, I returned to South Africa as a single missionary. My assignment was filling in for missionary church planters while they were on home ministry. I don't think it would have mattered much if I were in Cape Town or Canada. Location wasn't the issue, but rather, how did I adjust to being a single interim pastor?

Living conditions: My accommodations were excellent. I didn't really need three bedrooms, but I did need to eat. At first I bought too much. Fruit and vegetables looked sad before I ate them up. The spaghetti I made lasted a week, and eating cold cereal and sandwiches tired fast.

Church friends accused me of being helpless and hopeless at housekeeping—not encouraging words. I just tried to get by with the bare essentials. Why should I make my bed in the morning when I had to pull the covers down again at night to get in? Louise had never faulted my dishwashing and vacuuming skills, but I was forced to add to my repertoire of domestic chores.

In the area of laundry, I learned the washer works fine as long as I remember to empty my pockets before starting the machine. One week I left a ballpoint pen in a dress-shirt pocket. Someone ought to invent washing machines equipped with scanners.

Social occasions: I was nervous and uncomfortable about showing hospitality. I did not dare invite people to eat my cooking! (I have too much respect for life to do that.) Not having people come for meals eliminated opportunities to get to know individuals and build the relationships that are so important as a pastor.

I was afraid of single women. I knew it was no time to even consider a new relationship with all the grief baggage I was carrying.

Ministry: I agree with the apostle Paul that the elder/pastor should be the "husband of one wife." A wife brings safety and balance to the pastorate. She makes sure you dress properly and critiques your messages. Louise played the piano and organ and sang in the choir. She was a teacher by profession and loved to teach. I think she was more valuable to a church than I was. The new church plants and I both lost the blessing of my wife's presence.

More important than housekeeping and ministry skills, however, I missed a human touch, a kiss, and a hug. A pillow doesn't provide much tactile response. A door jam doesn't give quite the same massage that soothing fingers do. Gaining experience in the learning-to-live-again category has no adequate substitute for what I had so often taken for granted. To the married person reading this, I say, "Go give your spouse a big kiss."

Adjusting: When my life changed, I struggled to find ways to spend my leisure hours. I read or watched the news or sports.

Socializing helped me adjust to my new reality. I found I needed to take the initiative and telephone one or two friends to see if we could get together. Our entertainment was simple and unsophisticated: a meal out, a game of Uno®, or just sitting around solving the world's problems.

I had to learn to give all my cares to my heavenly Father. That does not mean that I never planned ahead or thought about my situation, but I tried not to fume, fuss, or lose sleep over it. My Father knows me—and my needs—so why should I worry? I did what I could and trusted God with what I was unable to do.

Over the years I have tried personally and have encouraged others to cast their burdens and anxieties on the Lord. *"Cast your burden on the LORD, and He shall sustain you"* (Psalm 55:22). *"Casting all your care upon Him; for He cares for you"* (1 Peter 5:7).

In adjusting to my new life as a single, I had plenty of opportunities to practice casting my cares on the Lord. And God has proven that He is sufficient.

Jeannie: Whether single, or married, or single again, we who are involved in Christian service hold many things in common. We are all striving to carry out God's plan and purpose for our lives. We have similar hopes, goals, and aspirations. Thus, stressing points of common interest and sharing ideas on how they can be implemented would be far more productive than dwelling on those which perpetuate a dichotomy among missionary personnel.

How much better it is to bridge gaps: between younger and older, between men and women, and between the married and the unmarried.

But how do we do this? It's not enough just to recognize problems in interpersonal relationships, or to theorize about how to avoid or handle them when they arise. A clear understanding of the potential for such problems is the first step.

SO, WHAT IS THE PROBLEM?

In my experience—and that of people I have talked with—the problem, while perhaps not actually stated, involves the subtle criticism and misunderstanding that occurs when singles and marrieds try to impose their values and priorities on each other. How easy it is for both sides to be insensitive. The issue seems to fall into the following three areas:

- *Perception:* This is the concept that all a person needs is to change his or her marital status and all will be well.

   An example of this occurred when I asked a mission leader about a mutual friend who had not been well. His answer: "She's suffering from single girl woes. You know, she's weepy and whiney. She just needs a husband." The young woman was later diagnosed with a serious chronic illness.

- *Opportunities:* In some organizations, mission fields, or educational institutions, work assignments are delegated according to gender or marital status. Academic achievement and experience are not taken into consideration.

   For example, in 2003–2004, Wally and I taught in Bible colleges in various African countries. One group hoped to open a church-based Bible institute. Among the missionary pool were two unmarried women, seasoned teachers then working on doctoral degrees. They could have organized, administered, and taught many of the courses, but that wasn't allowed. Instead, a pastor with no teaching experience was appointed as administrator, and the women were assigned to youth ministry.

- *Attitude:* Some singles are unduly preoccupied with their singleness. It may indeed be their present state of being, but there is no need to make it the focal point of their existence. A person who is comfortable with singleness can afford to laugh about being single or any other topic. And there are thousands of better topics to laugh about.

Of course, just laughing about your singleness is not the way to handle problems. Throughout the book we'll discuss the advantages and disadvantages of "whatever state you are in," as the apostle Paul wrote. Laughter, however, is indeed a "good medicine."

TIME DOESN'T CHANGE EVERYTHING

As I started the revision of the third edition of this book, I thought, *Surely things have changed since I first wrote about the singles/doubles issue. We live in a politically correct society where words are chosen carefully.*

But some things apparently have not changed. Early in 2008, our annual trip teaching in Bible colleges took us to a country where two delightful twenty-something missionary women, Joy and Lyza, had recently arrived. They volunteered the information that, indeed, they were called "single girls" while they were raising their support team. They also had been told: "Singles find it harder than couples to get support."

These two blew that idea away. With the help of a supportive pastor and creative ideas, both of them arrived in their place of service in an uncommonly short time.

Joy said that many churches where she spoke regarded her as a hero for going on her own!

Lyza ran into a bit of an awkward situation concerning her commissioning service. (This is a special service the home church conducts to pray for—and commission—the new missionary.) Lyza explained, "I was the first missionary girl to go out from my church. They were only used to an ordination service for a man entering full-time ministry. They really didn't know what to do with a woman. I knew how a commissioning service could be conducted but didn't feel free to share these ideas. By God's grace, it turned out to be a beautiful, God-honoring service."

Lyza also ran up against the stereotype that single women have a harder time both on pre-field ministry and in their place of service than a married couple have. She recalls, "While phoning to set up meetings, a pastor asked me, 'What has been the hardest thing you have or will face as a single woman going to the mission field?'

"I told him kindly, 'I think the hardest thing is the perception from pastors that the process will be harder for me as a single woman than it would be for a married couple. Married life and single life both have advantages and disadvantages.

'It is true there are struggles a single woman—or man—will face that a married couple will not face, but there are also many struggles married couples face that a single person does not encounter. The struggles of one are not better or worse than the other, they are just different.

'At this time in life, I know the Lord has called me to be single. As long as I am single I plan to enjoy the ministry and personal advantages of the single life and not get focused on the disadvantages.' The pastor liked my answer and the church invited me to speak."

Lyza also gave a plus side of raising support as a single woman when she said, "I would not have realized how much I love speaking to an audience. With a husband, I would have let him do the speaking and perhaps not shared my own passion."

Joy remarked, "I don't feel I lack a place on the team because I'm single." Both women, however, felt that married missionaries may have false assumptions about what will be a single woman's major area of outreach. "They usually think you will work with children," she said. Both Joy and Lyza enjoy children but feel their gifts are more in counseling, discipleship, and teaching the Bible to adults.

Such problems are not insurmountable, and the following chapters offer some principles which, I trust, if put into practice, can lead to harmony in living and working together.

The aim of this book is to foster better working, living, and growing relationships among people who have been placed together by an organization, a mission agency, and God Himself. Most of my examples come from Bangladesh and India because that is the part of the world with which I'm most familiar. And I want to state to the glory of God and the praise of the ABWE–Bangladesh missionary team that we have had a minimum of conflict in the singles/marrieds area, and we hear upbeat reports from other parts of the world, also.

BETWEEN THE LINES

Tribute to a Single Woman Missionary
from a Married Male Colleague

Agnes Haik is just "Aggie" to her colleagues and hundreds of Brazilians. During more than twenty years of service in Brazil, she helped start churches, taught in Bible schools, and was involved with camp and youth ministries. Aggie is known for her warm personality, infectious humor, and gracious hospitality. She always looks for ways to help people.

Thanks to her, many Brazilian young men and women, who were her "kids," have grown up and taken their places in leadership roles. When she felt her work in Brazil was finished, Aggie became a counselor for ABWE's Mobilization Department. This involved traveling to many schools and churches to share her enthusiasm for missions.

Aggie had a positive attitude toward her singleness. She loved to be a part of the couples' lives and spend time with the missionary kids. Her leadership skills and varied activities meant she often worked with the male missionaries. Aggie interacted very comfortably with the husbands and showed a sincere interest in their work. Wives, too, felt very comfortable around her. Neither the husbands nor the wives were ever made to feel threatened by Aggie. She contributed much to our team. Aggie was a great single missionary.

—Frank Bale, missionary to Brazil and Portugal,
Former Director of ABWE–Canada

Even good situations, however, hold room for improvement. There may be a need for clearer understanding, for ways to prevent breakdowns in interpersonal communication, or for mutual sensitivity as to remarks and situations which cause friction.

As we look into various situations, we will switch back and forth from unmarrieds to marrieds in order to relate to each group more fully. Also, at the end of each chapter, I will add areas and situations in life that I am working through since initially writing *By Ones and By Twos.*

LIFE'S LESSONS I'M TRYING TO LEARN

TO MARRY OR NOT TO MARRY?

Between the second and third editions of this book, I crossed from the singles' to the doubles' game. For some of the years before that, I spent time ("wasted" may be a better word) pleading with God to get this or that man saved, called into ministry, or make him willing to go into career foreign missions. I sometimes shudder to think what might have happened if God had answered those prayers.

Soon after my marriage, I gave my testimony as part of a series of talks at the annual Empire State Women's Advance Conference. Since Wally was conducting a seminar on "Helping Hurting People," he was one of the few men in the audience. I came to the part where I said, "God knew what was best for me. All along, He knew that 'old Wally was waiting in the wings.'" Wally's face reddened as 500 women turned to look at him.

What if there had been no Wally? I like Daniel chapter three as an answer. The three Jewish captives refused to worship the image of King Nebuchadnezzar. They knew God was able to deliver them. Then comes verse 18, "But if not . . ." and their promise to stay true to God and His plan for their lives no matter what.

At the time I met Wally, I was content with my life as a single. Newly returned from Bangladesh, I was on the staff at the ABWE International Headquarters. For the first time in my adult life I had my own home and all my worldly possessions in one place. I had located a fine church and had both old and new friends around me. Now I am content as a happily married woman. One state is not better than the other; each is "best" within the will of God.

The following excerpts from the Foreword of *Recovering Biblical Manhood and Womanhood** by Wayne Grudem and John Piper offer helpful insights:

1. **Marriage is not the final destiny of any human being** (Mark 12:25).

   In the resurrection, marriage—as we know it—will not exist. Love will be transposed into a key above and beyond marriage in this life, and having been single here will prove to be no disadvantage in eternity.

2. **Jesus Christ, the most fully human person who ever lived, was not married** (John 10:10).

   Cheryl Forbes, author of *Women of Devotion Through the Centuries*, wrote: "Jesus is the example to follow. He was single. . . . He had deep friendships among all sorts of people: men and women, single and married. Jesus allowed himself to be interrupted by needy children, distraught fathers, hungry men, and sick women.

3. **The Bible celebrates celibacy because it gives extraordinary opportunity for single-minded investment in ministry for Christ** (1 Corinthians 7:32).

   David Brainerd, missionary to the American Indians (1718–1747) said, "I cared not where or how I lived, or what hardships I went through, so that I could but gain souls for Christ. While I was asleep I dreamed of these things, and when I awoke the first thing I thought of was this great work. All my desire was for the conversion of the heathen, and all my hope was in God."

4. **The apostle Paul and a lot of great missionaries after him have renounced marriage for the sake of the kingdom of God** (Matthew 19:12).

This renunciation has, in many cases, required immense courage and devotion to Christ.

Mary Slessor worked in the interior of West Africa at the end of the nineteenth century and deeply desired a companion. Her hope centered on Charles Morrison, a fellow missionary on the coast. They were engaged, but the mission would not allow him to transfer to the interior because of his poor health. She would have to move to Duke Town along the Calabar River. She wrote: "It is out of the question. To leave an interior place like Okoyong without a worker and go to one of a dozen places where people have an open Bible and plenty of privilege! It is absurd. If God does not send him here, then he must do his work, and I must do mine where we have been placed."

5. **The apostle Paul calls singleness a gift from God** (1 Corinthians 7:7).

Jesus says in Matthew 19:12: *"The one who can accept this should accept it."*

Ada Lum, well-known author and trainer with International Christian Students Fellowship, admits that accepting singleness as a gift was a process for her. "For a long time I did not consider my single status a gift from the Lord. I did not resent it—to be frank—in my earlier idealistic period I thought that because I had chosen singleness I was doing God a favor! But in later years I was severely tested again on that choice. Through Paul's words and life, and my experiences, it gently dawned on me that God had given me a superb gift!"

6. **God is sovereign over who marries and who doesn't** (Romans 8:32).

God rules in these affairs, and we will be happier when we bow before His inscrutable ways. And He can be trusted to do what is good for those who trust in Him.

---

*Taken from the Preface of *Recovering Biblical Manhood and Womanhood*, edited by Wayne Grudem and John Piper © 1991. Used by permission of Crossway Books, a division of Good News Publishers, Wheaton, IL 60187, www.crossway.com.

CHAPTER 2

The Know-it-all

At the close of a board meeting at a Christian organization, a national man remarked, "I wish that once—only once—when I ask a question, a missionary would admit, 'I don't know.'"

What did he mean? Just this: As a group, missionaries tend to be achievers. Sometimes, with all their education, specialized training, and degree of expertise, missionaries begin to act as if they are omniscient. This insightful national Christian leader saw right through it.

Of course, in this age of specialization and ever-increasing knowledge, no one can ever possibly "know it all." And when we do need to know something, a click on the Internet will get the information we need. We have found this to be true in Internet cafés in places such as Ulaan Bataar, Mongolia, and Chiang Rai, Thailand. Even those who are well informed should guard against appearing to be a walking encyclopedia.

 To the unmarried: It may be you had more opportunities for formal education and earned more degrees than your married missionary sisters. It is important not to assume you are the final authority on all subjects, even if you do have a string of letters after your name. Women with less formal education might have more practical experience through work situations, counseling others, or rearing children. Listen to them, and don't lightly discount suggestions based on wisdom and experience.

To the married: Probably most of your time is spent in being a homemaker. Rather than deciding you have special know-how in this field, it is good to remember that housekeeping, home decorating, and cooking are skills anyone can learn. As in every sphere, some people have a flair for certain aspects that makes them outstanding where others are mediocre. That flair can apply to any person—married or not.

The first time I presented this singles/marrieds topic, missionary Cathy Kendall provided an illustration. At my candidate class, Cathy was in charge of the kitchen. She planned the meals and baked the cinnamon coffee cake and feather-light dinner rolls for which she was famous. The next time I saw Cathy was in her home on the outskirts of Manila, where she was acting dean of women at Baptist Bible Seminary and Institute. Her living quarters, though small, were tastefully arranged; in every sense of the word hers was a home, a place where students felt welcome to talk over their concerns or just relax. Then she married. Since her marriage, I've had the pleasure of being entertained by her and found her the same gracious hostess and excellent cook that she was as a single. Unmarried women can share tips about cooking and housekeeping to married women, and vice-versa.

The same is true regarding caring for children. The biological fact of giving birth does not necessarily make a woman a good mother. Think of Amy Carmichael, of Gladys Aylward, and of scores of unknown women who have been wonderful mothers, although they never had children of their own. Natural parenthood does not guarantee a built-in knowledge of children's needs and how to meet them.

THE POWER OF WORDS

"You wouldn't know anything about this; you don't have children." That phrase is sometimes thoughtlessly tossed out by married people; it can cause pain to the unmarried. The one being spoken to may, in fact, have a world of experience with children. Or—even more painful—the possibility of not bearing children may be the hardest trial of a woman's not being married. To have this rubbed in by careless words is cruel. Most women assume they will marry and have children. When it appears that those dreams will not be realized, there is generally enough disappointment without reminders through either careless or deliberate remarks.

Parents, please try to accept gracefully suggestions concerning your children. This is especially important if the people teaching your children are single. Once I heard a woman explaining one reason she had chosen the mission agency under which she and her husband planned to serve: "In this mission I'll be allowed to teach my own children, and not have to turn them over to some single missionary who never had children of her own." Such a speech can destroy good relationships.

There may be times when, married or not, you really do know more about the subject under discussion than others present. I would hope your colleagues will be wise and mature enough to take your knowledge and expertise into account. But, usually, unless your contribution is requested, it is wise to keep your know-how to yourself.

We are all acquainted with individuals who love to hear themselves talk. No matter the topic, they have something to say. They butt into conversations. They deflate a person by following his story with, "Oh, that's nothing. You should hear what happened to me. . . ." They ruin conversation by monopolizing it. Wise was the person who wrote,

It's better to keep your mouth shut
And have people think you are ignorant,
Than to open it—and remove all doubt.

Remember Peter on the Mount of Transfiguration as recorded in Matthew 17:1–8? Impulsive Peter could not just bask in the awe and glory of the experience; he had to say something. What he blurted out was a real gem: *"It is good for us to be here,"* and God cut him short. *"While he thus spoke . . . ,"* God said, *"this is my beloved Son: hear Him."* God is too polite to be vulgar, but a loose translation of His rebuke would be something like, "Shut up, Peter, and listen for once!"

A TIMELY WORD

Sometimes our words spoil our good intentions, as, for example, when we go to comfort someone in trouble or bereavement. Instead of just being there, perhaps sitting with an arm around our friend, we have to talk. And the words we say! "I understand." "I know how you feel." Unless we have been through an identical experience, we cannot possibly understand the pain our friend is feeling.

Wally experienced this after the deaths of his wife and daughter, Louise and Ruth. Well-meaning friends quoted Bible verses such as, "All things work together for good. . . ." A marvelous verse, but Wally couldn't understand how "things were working together for good" as he stood beside two coffins. In the "Helping Hurting People" seminars he conducts worldwide, Wally advises people to think before they open their mouths and not ask self-serving, curiosity questions such as, "What happened?" "Did you get a second opinion from another doctor?" "What makes of cars were involved?" (Does it really matter if you were struck by a Ford or a Toyota?) He suggests just being there for your grieving friend, perhaps giving a hug or holding a hand. When you don't know what to say, say nothing:

"When the grief is the newest,
Let your words be the fewest."

LEARNING FROM EXPERIENCE

New missionaries especially have to guard against knowing and saying it all, and here I speak from bitter experience. I was young when I arrived in Chittagong, a new R.N. with two-and-a-half additional years at Cedarville College (now University) where I earned a B.Sc. degree. I grew up in a pastor's home where missionaries and heads of missions visited frequently. The question between my older brother, Bruce, and me when we moved to a new house was, "Do you want the bigger bedroom you have to give up for the missionaries or the little one you can keep for yourself?"

Attending missionary conferences, especially the "King of Conferences" at People's Church in Toronto, Canada, was a highlight of my childhood. I still recall the curio tables with scorpions in bottles and booklets written in exotic languages. I had taught children since I was a child of eight myself. I had sung and "said missionary pieces" in churches and conferences throughout the United States and Canada.

Oh yes, I knew all about being a missionary. I knew what to do and what everyone else ought to do also. And what's more, I said it—vociferously! I scorned the practice of household help. I vowed I would do all my cooking and cleaning myself, thank you. I objected to the rule of a solid year of language study without being allowed active ministry. I criticized what was being offered to the missionary children for their spiritual growth.

It took a long time—too long—to bring me down from the notion that I had all the answers. My colleagues lovingly and patiently helped me understand the "whys" behind the policies and practices. Together we worked out programs that were mutually beneficial. But many times since those days, I've wished I had just kept quiet.

For some of us, speaking our mind is a problem we have to work on our entire lives. My housemate of more than twenty-five years, Lynn Silvernale, bore the brunt of much of my tendency to speak my mind. One evening as Lynn and I returned from a meeting our neighbors greeted us saying, "You had a visitor from the hospital . . ."

Without waiting to hear the details, I started in with, "Why did they come tonight? They wrote that they were coming tomorrow. Why can't people do what they say they are going to do?"

I noticed Lynn was trying to say something, but I barged ahead, "Where will they sleep? We don't have anything ready. Why didn't they let us know?" When I stopped for a breath, our neighbor enlightened me that the person who came unexpectedly had nothing to do with the guests I was talking about. Later, I asked Lynn why she hadn't told me I had made a mistake.

She replied, "I didn't think it was worth it. You already had your mind made up."

That was another one of the many times when I would have done well to remember the Chinese proverb: "Closed mouths gather no feet."

THE WISDOM TO LISTEN

By contrast, four years after my arrival in Bangladesh, Jesse and Joyce Eaton, a couple with pastoral experience in the United States, joined our team. At their first business meeting, a point of church polity related to a cross-cultural situation arose. Jess was asked his opinion. He replied, "I think we'll just listen this time." What a wise man!

Please don't misunderstand. I am not saying that new missionaries should be seen but not heard. Any organization that does not allow new ideas, new patterns of learning, or new methods of outreach, will stagnate. Any group that operates on the principle that "we've always done it this way" is doomed. Sometimes the greenest recruit brings new insights unknown to the rest of the team. Sometimes the newcomer has been exposed to approaches that worked elsewhere and might work well in this situation. New thoughts, new ideas, and new people are welcome. It is the attitude in which the newness is clothed that is important. A humble attitude that suggests (not insists); a concern that asks, "What do you think about this?" "Have you read about . . . ?" will produce much better results than my bull-in-the-china-shop approach. It all goes back to the opening words in this chapter, being willing to admit, "I don't know," rather than acting as though we know it all.

ADVICE TO A BRIDE

The guests at my bridal shower were told to write notes of advice they thought would be helpful for this mid-50s bride. Here's a helpful one: "We'll never understand how it is that these brilliant men we marry can't locate the laundry basket."

I found most of the rest of the suggestions apply equally to men or women, married or single:

- People are able to change; in most cases they never do. If you go into a relationship expecting to make over your spouse or housemate, forget it. You're doomed before you ever start.
- Appreciate the differences in one another.
- Pray daily for the grace to overlook one another's faults.
- Blessed are the flexible for they shall never be bent out of shape.

CHAPTER 3

Part of a Family

Psalm 68:6 tells us that "God sets the solitary in families." This beautiful verse has deep meaning for those far from their homelands.

Cross-cultural missionaries live in two worlds. For two, three, or four years at a stretch their home is in a foreign country and culture. Yes, they try to keep up with families and friends by email, websites, blogs, letters, and phone calls; but life goes on without them. Nieces and nephews are born, star in school productions, graduate, and marry. When missionaries return to their own families and friends, they often feel like outsiders.

Gradually, however, the missionary finds a new home with those among whom he has come to live and work. In his place of ministry, a person may live in close contact with a wide range of people: longtime missionaries, new recruits, and their children. All speak the same language—both literally and figuratively. Each one lives through the same frustrations, weathers the same crises, and, it is to be hoped, grows to be long-suffering towards one another's quirks.

This sense of belonging is seen so clearly when people from the same mission field meet in their home countries. This scenario has happened to me many times: A tall teenager bounds across his college campus with an unembarrassed "Hey, Aunt Jeannie!"—and we talk our heads off getting caught up on news from Bangladesh.

Once when I had been in North America for about eight months of a year's furlough ministry, an assignment from the mission office brought together six of us from Bangladesh. One young woman rushed up, hugged me, and said, "A year ago, if anyone had told me I'd be happier to see you than to see my own sisters, I would have said they were crazy. But it's true. We each know what the other means. We can talk together." And we did!

Another woman expressed, "I love my own family dearly, but when I need help in thinking through decisions, I feel I have to share the problem with someone from my missionary family."

"God sets the solitary in families": You may be a prospective missionary who doesn't have a warm relationship with your biological family. Wait until you are settled in your place of ministry. You can have a beautiful family relationship—as long as you are willing to love and nurture it.

BROTHERS AND SISTERS, WITH BOUNDARIES

While on the mission field, missionaries often assume the kinship relationship of brother and sister with the responsibilities and privileges afforded by those terms. Relationships are all-important, especially in an Eastern culture where everyone, it seems, is related to everyone else. In the East you find relationship terms and corresponding roles for people as far removed as your brother's son's wife's parents. A person in isolation is an anomaly in Asia and other parts of the world and is seen as someone to be pitied. The concept is that even society's outcasts have some relatives to fall back on, so we become our colleagues' figurative brothers and sisters. And are we not, in fact? As children of the same heavenly Father, we are brothers and sisters in Christ.

Circumstances have arisen (as during wartime) when a mixed group found themselves in very close living quarters, where they all had to spend the night in the same room, or when the call of nature must be answered in primitive surroundings. All of this is easier to explain to questioning eyes and easier to laugh off yourself if you think of your fellow worker as a big—or little—brother or sister.

A missionary husband may have a policy about riding in cars or holding meetings alone with any woman other than his wife. This may be a wise policy to protect his marriage, yet each region of the world has different standards of proper behavior. Some cultures do not view it as strange when men and women who are not married to each other travel together on business. For example, Donna Messenger, who served with ABWE in Ukraine, said, "The national pastors wondered why a male teammate would leave me to walk back alone from the Bible Institute to my apartment, while he drove himself home. To them, the danger of my walking alone was greater than any danger of my being alone in the car with him."

INVESTING IN RELATIONSHIPS

We who are missionaries usually consider ourselves as part of a family or a team. If we accept the pleasures of belonging to a large family, we must also be willing to accept the obligations entailed: loyalty, concern, assistance—which can all be summed up in the word "love." Romans 12:10 admonishes that we be devoted to one another in brotherly love.

At times, this will mean carefully watching our words and not divulging business to those outside the family. It may mean sticking our necks out for somebody when he is in trouble. It always means showing at least the same respect and affection for colleagues as we show—or ought to show—to our own brothers and sisters.

Just as in your home country, it may be that in your place of service you "click" more with one person, couple, or family than with others. That is natural, but try to get to know all the people with whom you live and work. This takes effort. It takes spending time together, both in working situations and especially in off-duty hours. It means doing thoughtful little things for one another.

I never was much good at throwing out mementos, so I still have a note from our senior missionary's wife, Beth Gurganus, addressed jointly to Lynn and me:

> Today, on my birthday, I was reminiscing about the goodness and greatness of God, and some of the highlights of my life passed through my mind. One of those was the birthday when you two appeared at my door to take me for a surprise ride. Do you remember? I had just washed my hair. We rushed around to find a hair dryer. Then we drove to the newly opened hotel for high tea in the coffee shop. That was lovely and is among my fond memories.

Every member of the missionary family can work at creating warm memories and building traditions. Anything we can do to nurture good feelings among fellow workers is worthwhile. The Bible gives good counsel concerning relationships:

> *For you, brethren, have been called to liberty; only do not use liberty as an opportunity for the flesh, but through love serve one another. For all the law is fulfilled in one word, even in this: "You shall love your neighbor as yourself." But if you bite and devour one another, beware lest you be consumed by one another!* (Galatians 5:13–15).

Lasagna Under Glass

One year the single missionaries gave a Valentine's Day party for the missionary couples living in Chittagong. We held the party in schoolteacher Sue Breckley's living room, which was decorated with the appropriate hearts and flowers. As the guests arrived, Lynn entertained them by playing sentimental songs on a small portable organ. The waiters then seated the couples at candlelit tables for two. Who were the waiters? Our missionary bachelor, Reid Minich, and Bob Morris, an American engineer who accepted Christ during his time in Chittagong. They looked the part perfectly with their black bow ties and white towels draped over their arms. Bob had menus printed with every exotic dish we could think of: *pâté de foie gras*, pheasant under glass, and many more. The two men walked from table to table, solemnly writing down the diners' choices. Then they came to the kitchen, where Sue and I dished up lasagna, the only dish prepared. The waiters took back the steaming squares with the apology, "Sorry, we are all out of Cornish hen (or whatever the order was), but would you like to try the house specialty?"

I moved from table to table singing songs that were meant especially for each couple—the songs contained lines with the wife's name or had a tune from their home place such as "Mary" or "Carolina Moon." Some songs had to be fudged a bit, as in the case of "Hello, Carol!"

We singles arranged for babysitters, and borrowed films from the U.S. Information Service to round out the evening. Yes, it took time out of our regular duties, but it was worth it. Those couples still talk about that expression of love and appreciation.

AUNTS AND UNCLES

If we missionaries are brothers and sisters, what does that make us to the kids? It makes us aunts and uncles.

"Auntie." How I hated that expression during my first years of missionary service. I must have driven people crazy showing my distaste for what—to them—was a natural term. But I had reason to dislike it. In my growing-up years, many, many visitors passed through our house. Some of these people wanted to be called "aunt" or "uncle," or else my parents didn't know any better term to use, so I acquired many aunts and uncles. To this day there are people whom I never call by name because I don't know what to call them. To say "Rev. Hunt" to a family friend would be stilted and formal, and for me to say "Uncle George" now sounds ridiculous. So I felt I had good reason not to lead another generation into the same problems I had faced. But I came to realize the value behind the practice of children calling adults "aunt" and "uncle."

Kids benefit from "adopted" aunts and uncles. They are away from their own relatives and need this relationship. And aunts and uncles need kids, too.

Living in close contact with families, unmarried people have the joy of sharing in family life: holding new babies, watching little ones take their first steps, and introducing helpful dimensions into the children's lives.

There's also a practical reason for using these terms. In many countries, local people are horrified hearing a small child call an adult by his first name. This simply is not done. At the same time, calling someone you interact with regularly Mr., Mrs., or Miss gets a little ridiculous. Using "aunt" and "uncle" solves the problem.

In much of Asia, even adults adopt respectful ways to address their elders. Since 2001, Wally and I have spoken and taught in India nearly every year. Among our dear friends are a highly respected pastor and his wife. Since they are still relatively young, they refer to us as Pastor and Auntie. That Indian pastor overheard a young Indian doctor address a senior missionary by his first name and responded, "Come on, have you forgotten you're Indian?" As pleasant and helpful as this family relationship can be, problems can arise, and cautionary flags may need to be raised.

To the unmarried: Love the missionary kids as you do your own nieces and nephews. Spend time with them. Offer to take care of them so that their parents can go out. You may want to have children's toys, games, and books at your house. By keeping these on a special bookshelf or in a toy box, children know they are welcome at your home. They will realize you thought about them and planned for their visits. In establishing a play area, however, you will want to have some rules. Those may include setting specific times when children can come. That prevents untimely running in and out or your feeling that people are taking advantage of you. If you have items you don't want touched, explain that to older children and "baby proof" the room for little ones by removing fragile objects. If you don't want a musical instrument in your house played or certain appliances turned on, tell the children. Make sure they know their limits. Expect children to abide by your rules while in your house. You are the adult, and this is your home.

In many aspects of living, but perhaps more in the area of caring for children, the rule "know your place" applies. Certain areas fall exclusively within the rights of parents, and anyone else does well to back away gracefully. Never correct or discipline a child when his own parents are present. If the rules of your house are broken, remove the offending item or focus of trouble, tell the parents if need be, but don't punish someone else's child. Parents have their own standards and rules of conduct. No outsider has the right to interfere.

But singles can volunteer when their help is needed. In 1971 Bangladesh underwent a civil and then an international war. All but three of the ABWE missionaries were required to evacuate the country (as were most missionaries from other agencies). My group of thirteen adults and twenty-one children traveled by Land Rover, sampan, army truck, PT boat, and plane on our route from Bangladesh through Burma and down to Bangkok, Thailand. But that's all another story. You can read more about this in the book *On Duty in Bangladesh.**

I remember at one holding point during our trip, American Embassy personnel came to our rescue with food and cold drinks. As we three singles, Becky Davey, Lynn Silvernale, and I, helped corral the children onto the next means of transport, an Embassy attaché remarked, "These kids obey you as if you were their parents."

Later, at the C&MA guest home in Bangkok where we lived as refugees for a few weeks, the kindly guest house manager would ask us, "What planned activity do you have for the children today?"—which meant, "When will we have a little peace around here?" The children did respond to us. We had then, and still have, a happy relationship with them even though they were not our own children, and we were careful not to put them in a position where their parents' standards and principles were questioned.

In spiritual areas, too, it would be wrong to usurp the parents' place. A group of Bangladesh missionaries was worshiping to-gether at a Sunday evening service in another country. During the meeting, a number of school children returning from their year in a boarding school gave testimonies of what God had done in their lives. Various ones told of accepting Christ as Savior or of winning spiritual victories. Each one praised the teachers, staff, and house-

---

**On Duty in Bangladesh*, by Jeannie Lockerbie, 1973, Zondervan Corporation. Now available through ABWE Publishing.

parents for the part those people had in their lives. Followin service, a young mother in our group wistfully said, "I wan. to have those experiences with my children myself."

I don't think she was being selfish. I think she was speaking for her God-given right and duty. God had given this family three children. The responsibility for their spiritual birth and growth is as important—or more so—as the children's physical development. That does not mean there will never be times when the housemother, the teacher, the auntie, or the uncle is not the right person to talk with the child. Sometimes distance, communication difficulties, or the emergency of the situation will demand that the person at hand be the one to guide the child. But when the child's own parents are present, they are the ones who should have the privilege of leading their children to Christ, teaching them God's design for love, sex, and marriage, and guiding them in decision making for the future.

To the married: Try never just to assume that an "auntie" or "uncle" will take care of your kids. Never take it for granted that single people don't have much to do, so of course they can babysit. Wait for them to offer or, if the singles don't know you need a babysitter, ask if it is possible for them to help. Even if a single is usually willing to care for your children, allow him or her to say "no" occasionally without your getting offended.

Sometimes unmarried people invite children to their homes without their parents. This can be a special treat for both: the kids get to eat out, and the parents get an evening to themselves! Over the years, traditions have been made this way. For example, on one mission station the children always go to the single women's house for an evening of Christmas cookie baking. One busy nurse tries to keep Sunday afternoons free to read to the younger MKs at the hospital where she and their parents work. Another group organizes an annual Valentine's Day party. Often, missionary men arrange sporting activities. Some MKs start playing soccer almost as soon as they can walk.

"Children are a heritage from the Lord," Proverbs tells us. Whether they are your own or those you have adopted by joining a mission family, they are precious. Children enrich the lives of everyone. One of the extras that I didn't expect when I signed up for Christian ministry is the joy of close association with children in my extended missionary family.

LIFE'S LESSONS I'M TRYING TO LEARN

THREE IMPORTANT WORDS

Considering yourself as part of a family goes a long way toward fostering better working and living relationships among Christian workers. What are three of the most important words in creating and maintaining good interpersonal relationships? "I love you" and "Thanks so much" rate high on the list. The best threesome I've heard, however, are words often quoted by our longtime pastor friend Dr. Gerry Benn.

Rather than pontificating on his subject, he prefaces startling truth, new insights, or answers to difficult questions with the words: "Just a thought . . ."

CHAPTER 4

Learning To Be Content

From time to time I have known an overwhelming sense of contentment. One instance happened during my second year as a missionary. My language teacher arrived for my 6:00 to 7:00 a.m. class. Never much of a morning person, I once again foggily recited my way through a reading assignment. By 8:00, ten squiggly preschoolers and kindergarteners arrived and perched on my front verandah for the nursery school I conducted so their parents could spend the morning in language study. If you've supervised ten under-fives all at once, you'll know the chaos of the morning. If you haven't, you wouldn't understand even if I told you.

Oh, well, I thought, *at least I can look forward to this evening.* My housemates and I had invited guests for dinner. Along with the meat and potatoes we had decided to serve, I had one hoarded tin of vegetables and a real treat: a cake mix only six months old from its voyage halfway around the world. I envisioned a chocolate layer cake with mounds of fluffy seven-minute frosting. At mid-morning—cookie and juice time—the cook called me to the kitchen. (Remember, I hadn't wanted that cook in the first place. Only when I learned that a woman does not usually do her own marketing in Bengali culture, and when I saw meat hanging by its haunches and live chickens flapping their wings in the market, did I realize the necessity for a cook.)

Wishing to surprise me and save me the work of making the cake and the frosting, the cook had prepared it himself and now called me to praise his handiwork. There on the counter sat my lovely cake. It lay in a long pan, as flat as the smoothest military sheet. And the icing! The toothless old cook grinned as he pointed to all the colors he had been able to conjure up out of four little food-coloring bottles. My white-mountain frosting had turned into Joseph's coat! Suspiciously, I lifted a lid from a pot on the stove. Boiling happily away was all the popcorn I had planned to pop for nibble food later in the evening. The cook complained it had been boiling for three hours, so why wasn't it getting soft?

A ruined cake, a houseful of squalling kids, and a lousy time for language study—life was awful! I let out one cry, "Lord, help me!" Suddenly, almost perceptibly, I was engulfed in comfort as the Lord seemed to say, "It's okay. I brought you here. I'll bring you through."

Then I started to laugh. Wait till the people tonight see that cake! And what a letter home the popcorn episode will make! I started back to the porch. Yes, Debbie and Mark were still fighting over the paintbrushes. Linda was mashing cookies all over the floor, and Marty was a mess; but it was all right. This was the place where I was supposed to be, and the work I was to do at this time. The Lord gave me His peace and contentment.

THE SOURCE OF CONTENTMENT

Where does contentment come from? Can it be worked up by fervent prayer and soul-searching? Is it handed out at conferences and retreats? Is it a spiritual grace to be sought? In my experience, the answer to each of these would be: "No."

Amy Carmichael, missionary to India for fify-five years, said it best: "In acceptance lies peace."

Acceptance is not maintaining "a stiff upper lip." Not a silly, "Praise the Lord, I broke my leg!" Not the pious tones we used at the cafeteria during my nurses' training days, when we prayed,

"Thank you Lord for these wretched powdered eggs." Rather, the acceptance that brings contentment is accompanied with gladness, as we read in both Psalms and Proverbs:

"You have put gladness in my heart" (Psalm 4:7).
"A merry heart does good like medicine" (Proverbs 17:22).

The world is full of frustrations over which a person, especially one living in a foreign country, has no control—endless government red tape; stifling bureaucracy that slows down every advancement; inefficiency brought on by an oppressive climate and poor health; shortages of water, electricity, and basic necessities; excessive rain or drought; and a host of other inconveniences. All of those can drive us to complain, retreat, or even quit altogether. Or, they can be taken in stride if underneath is the basic foundational belief that this is where God wants me to be. I can and will be happy here.

Andrew Murray (1828–1917), the son of missionaries, served in South Africa as a missionary pastor. His formula for a contented spirit:

I am here by God's appointment
In His keeping
Under His training
For His time.

The concept that I am in these circumstances by God's design must involve more than a grin-and-bear-it attitude. There must be joy in being and doing what God has called us to be and do. Without joy, the long hours become unendurable toil; the frustrations become misery. Christ said, *"I have come that they may have life, and that they may have it more abundantly"* (John 10:10). Satan tries to rob the Christian worker of his usefulness by destroying his sense of joy. Jesus prayed for you in John 16:24, "that your joy may be full."

Any Christian worker performing his duty simply out of obligation might do well to reevaluate his area of service. When God calls an individual to a place or a ministry, He strengthens that person with joy. That is not to imply that the road will always be smooth. No, the outward circumstances may be very hard. They may include pain, illness, separation from loved ones, and lack of interest from the people who promised support and prayer.

Even harder may be the disappointments in the work you have come to do. Others write about scores of souls saved, while the ones and twos you work with seem to be slipping backwards. In other countries, new churches spring up faster than the church growth charts; your struggling church is fractious and barely alive. You teach your heart out on matters of Christian living, only to have your finest leaders agree wholeheartedly, then remark that they will do what they are accustomed to doing. You exert yourself to raise a family from abject poverty. You treat them medically, locate employment, put their children in school, locate a better living environment—and the man of the house robs you blind! You labor over an inquirer, lead her to Christ, painstakingly guide her in her first steps, eventually breathe a sigh of relief as she seems firm and grounded in her faith, only to watch her slip back to her old religion for the expediency of a job or marriage.

These are not joyous experiences. They cause heartache, disappointment, and discouragement. Even in distressing conditions, however, there can be an underlying sense of contentment that says, "This place and these circumstances are right for me at this time." This must be more than head knowledge, more than lip service to a bunch of platitudes. It must be the fact upon which you build your life. The apostle Paul wrote, *"Godliness with contentment is great gain"* (I Timothy 6:6). Even Paul admitted this attitude does not come naturally. He said in Philippians 4:11, *"I have learned in whatever state I am, to be content."* Missionary Elizabeth

Elliot made this observation: "The secret is Christ in me, not me in a different set of circumstances."

One of the biggest obstacles to a life of contentment is envy of another person—his position, marital status, and opportunities. We never seem to envy another person's trials, do we? Yet these might well be what made that person who he is.

BETWEEN THE LINES

Learning to Accept

In her classic *Hind's Feet in High Places*, Hannah Hurnard gives excellent insights:

> "It is God's will that some of His children should learn deep union with Himself through the perfect flowering of natural human love in marriage. For others it is equally His will that the same perfect union should be learnt through the experience of learning to lay down completely this natural and instinctive desire for marriage and parenthood, and the circumstances of life which deny them this experience. . . . The only way is by learning to accept day by day, the actual conditions and tests permitted by God, by a continual repeated laying down of our own will and acceptance of His as it is presented to us in the form of the people with whom we have to live and work, and in the things that happen to us." [1]

Let's talk about the important issue of being content, whether married or unmarried.

 An unmarried woman may ask, "Why does she have somebody who loves her? Why does she have someone to take care of her while I don't?" These types of questions waste time and energy. Paul said unmarried people may be able to devote more time to ministry, but that's not true if you're constantly asking, "Why don't I have a wife/husband?" If you spend time complaining, scheming, and accusing God, that time Paul mentioned is dissipated in useless emotional energy.

The issue of marriage (or not), or the timing of marriage is best left in God's hands. In Psalm 47:4, David wrote, *"He will choose our inheritance for us."*

Charles H. Spurgeon (1834–1892), English preacher and author, expanded on this:

> "Had any other condition been better for you
>   than the one in which you find yourself,
>   divine love would have placed you there."

I get weary of stories like this: Girl says to God, "I will go to the mission field only if I have a husband." After a spiritual struggle she comes to the point of surrender where she says, "All right, Lord, I am willing to go to the mission field without a husband," and bingo—a husband appears! It's as if you get a lollipop or a goody sticker for having said, "I surrender to God."

If it is in God's plan for you to have a husband, God will arrange it. Remember, God loves you so much. Jeremiah 29:11 reinforces that assurance: *"I know the thoughts that I think toward you, says the Lord, thoughts of peace and not of evil, to give you a future and a hope."* Rather than frustrating yourself with trying to figure out the unfathomable "whys," cultivate peace and contentment. "Why" is a defeat-producing word. It gets you nowhere, like a dog chasing its own tail.

Above all, don't allow questions you cannot answer to strangle your joy and become a root of bitterness in your life.

BETWEEN THE LINES

Save Me from Bitterness

I first found the following poem signed "anonymously," then later credited to Natalie Ray. Read these poignant words carefully and take them to heart, especially if resentment toward God is eating away at you because you feel you have been refused what you think is your heart's desire.

No lover makes my kiss his daily quest.
No hand across the table reaches mine.
No precious baby nestles at my breast.
No one to need my love. Where is the sign
That God, my Father loves me? Surely He
Creates this wealth of love to overflow.
How can it be that no one who wanted me
Has become mine? Why did I tell them "no"?

But do they really matter—all the "Why's"?
Could all the answers take away the pain,
Or all the reasons really dry my eyes,
Though sent from Heaven's courts?
No, I would weep again.
My God, You have saved me from Hell's black abyss;
Oh, save me from the tyranny of bitterness!

A Wycliffe woman missionary in the Philippines is anything but bitter about her situation. She says, "I don't think being single is all that awful. I've certainly enjoyed it. But maybe I've been fortunate in that I have always had good friends in the same boat,

with none of us sitting around crying about it." That's contentment—with joy.

 In my experience, the married women's "whys" polarize at two
extremes. One says, "Why do I have to learn a foreign language?
I'm not going to preach and teach. I'll be taking care of my house
and family." Ginny DeVries, former missionary mother and Bible
translator in the Philippines, addressed this question as follows in
a talk called "A Matter of Motivation":

> "Fellow wives and mothers, I'd like to interject a special
> word about our part in this enterprise. When we joined the
> mission together with our husbands, we came with the full
> knowledge that we were coming as missionaries. Frankly, I
> think our job is harder than that of the men: We are called
> to be wives first, mothers second, and missionaries third. It
> is no easy matter to correlate these three roles. But the Lord
> has not asked us to do anything for which He will not
> empower us. If we were in our home countries, we'd be
> doing all our own cooking, cleaning, washing, and market-
> ing. If the Lord has provided us with household help, we
> will not be spending any less time with our children because
> of doing missionary work than we would be at home where,
> presumably, we do all the housekeeping.
>
> "Could it be that our language learning is attacked so
> fiercely because the devil knows we need to know it in order
> to be effective missionaries?"

Everyone knows it is difficult to leave those little ones while
you go to language school. It is hard to keep your mind on past
active participles when you have been up all night with a crying
baby. It may be heart-rending to send school-age children to
boarding school. Hard—yes; impossible—no. Mothers serving in
many countries testify how thankful they are that they were
encouraged—or forced—to spend extensive time in language

study when they first arrived in their place of service. One mother of four wrote, "Being a missionary mother and learning a new language will never be an easy or a comfortable thing, but it is necessary."

When a group of parents in Bangladesh were engrossed in Bengali language study, they were encouraged by missionaries studying Chinese in Hong Kong. The encouragement came in the form of a poem which we freely admit plagiarizing. Here is part of the Bengali adaptation:

"Rain is coming under the door,
Water's covered the bathroom floor.
It doesn't mean a thing to me.
Today's a quiz on lesson three.

Another bulb must be replaced
The baby's in my new toothpaste!
How can I do conversation?
And revise today's translation?

Home is 12,000 miles away
Frustrations multiply each day
When you're feeling glum and growly.
Forget it all—just learn Bengali."[2]

UNEXPECTED ASSETS

At the other end of the spectrum of asking "why," a married woman may say, "This isn't fair. God called me to be a missionary, too. I dedicated my life to serve the Lord. Why do I have to be stuck in this house all the time? All I ever do is take care of my kids."

This attitude can lead to as much bitterness as that of the woman with no children to care for. It could cause a mother to leave her children with unsuitable caregivers, where they might learn improper language and unsanitary or immoral practices. Or it may cause her to continually leave her children on a fellow worker's doorstep while she goes out to do "the Lord's work."

Again the solution to the problem boils down to "acceptance with joy" of the situation in which each woman finds herself. Children are little for such a short while—it is vital that mothers spend time with them. All too soon a mother finds that, when she wants to hold them or give them a hug, they are too grown up for all that "nonsense." Use your time wisely. When the children are sleeping, playing safely, or in school, you can engage in other activities.

Those children who some mothers may think of as "keeping me from missionary work" might actually turn out to be the biggest door-openers into national homes. When you take children along, or even talk about homemaking and rearing children, much of your initial introduction is over because you can immediately relate to local people on these issues you have in common.

Unmarried people sometimes have a harder time getting the conversation going when visiting in a new area. Invariably, people ask about family. The conversation goes like this: "What does your husband do? You don't have a husband! Have you no parents or relatives? Why did they not arrange a marriage for you?"

A colleague, Mary Lou Brownell, who served in Bangladesh for thirty years, has a classic answer. She sweetly replies, "My husband died at birth." For those who do not need such an excuse, praise God for your husband and children and for the opening they give into people's homes.

THE OTHER MAN; THE OTHER WOMAN

 The married missionary woman's frustrations may increase when the problem is compounded by another attitude: "I'm stuck here at home with these kids and some other woman is working with my husband." Here, words of caution are in order to all, single or married: *"Abstain from every form (all appearance) of evil"* (I Thessalonians 5:22).

When a woman is working with someone else's husband, or a man with someone else's wife, they both need to make sure that everything about the relationship is above board. Perhaps office doors should have windows, or be left open so people can see what is going on inside. Do not give cause for suspicion to the man's wife, the woman's husband, the national staff, or anyone else.

In Bangladesh and many other cultures, it is not considered possible for a person to live a pure moral life alone. So, when nationals see a man and woman in deep discussion or in close proximity, they assume the two are married or that somebody is up to no good.

Singles, more than likely, will be involved in projects with someone else's spouse as a nurse or doctor in a hospital or a teacher in a school, to mention just two situations. Men often get completely involved in their work. They forget that back home with the kids, half of the team hasn't heard about this project. The wives need to be included in the discussion and be allowed to give their ideas on matters of general concern.

Spouses must realize that, sometimes, teachers, doctors, and nurses do have to "talk shop" among themselves. It is a great help when the spouse who is not involved in the conversation is understanding and doesn't make a big deal when business matters must be discussed with colleagues. A spouse who is jealous without cause can break a good-working relationship. It's damaging to assume that because an unmarried colleague casually passes the time of day with your spouse, that colleague has designs on him or her. This is likewise true of a person who misreads normal working interaction as an indication that the other has ulterior motives.

If a husband or wife, however, feels they have cause to be concerned about a person's relationship with their spouse, they need to get to the root of the problem—fast. Talk it out first with your spouse. Or—if possible—talk with the "other" man or woman. If neither of these seems possible, call in a third party to mediate. Don't let Satan get the upper hand here. He would love to tear a marriage apart under the guise of two people dedicated to their work.

Donna Messenger adds this suggestion from her ministry in Ukraine: "I have had many occasions to work closely with married men. I always made it a point to develop a friendship with their wives so that in my own mind I view them as a couple."

A special word to the *men* is appropriate here. Sometimes actions or words you use can innocently get you into trouble. For example, in a shoe store in New York City, a man I'd never seen before called me "darling" as I walked in. In London, England, conductors on the underground warn passengers: "Mind the gap, love."

Endearing terms such as "honey" or "sweetheart" are often used without a second thought. In most countries, Hollywood movies are commonplace, and local people know what "honey," "darling," and "sweetheart" imply. When you say these words to someone other than your wife, listeners will be suspicious, however innocent you are. A good rule is to remove those words from your vocabulary for anyone outside your family.

In many countries, a man has to be careful even about the way he conducts himself with his wife in public. If it is seen as sexual to hold your wife's hand, imagine how the locals view hugging an unmarried co-worker! Social mores vary greatly from country to country. Here's a quote from a book of advice to expatriates living in Bangladesh: "Kissing is for children, for the bedroom, and for mad foreigners in the movies."

Some men are outgoing types who put an arm around a woman, or give her a pat in greeting. Beware of physical conduct with anyone but your own family. Besides how it may look to watching nationals, there is another reason for restraint: The woman you are calling "dear" or "sweetie-pie" or patting on the shoulder may be feeling particularly lonely. She may take your expression entirely the wrong way. You meant absolutely nothing by it. You might call the cat by the same term, but the girl might pick up your words or gestures and build something in her mind that you never intended.

LIVE IN THE NOW

Situations as a career Christian worker may be different from what you are used to. They may be funny or frustrating, unusual or unsettling. Whatever they are, your loving Lord chooses them for you at this time in your life. Did you notice that sentence is in the present tense? Too many people merely endure life now, existing in the vague hope that somehow things will be better in the future.

Many women turn down invitations to be part of a group attending a play, a concert, or a sports event because they don't have a date. Granted, it is delightful to have a special companion, but don't let the lack of one keep you home if the event is something you would enjoy. If the occasion interests you, go—even if it means going alone. Better to sit alone enjoying the program than to sit alone at home. Do what you enjoy. Do it now. Don't wait until some dim, distant future when your circumstances might have changed.

Buy or make what is necessary to create a home. Use your own abilities or borrow the skills of a friend. Don't fall into the mind-set that thinks, "If this were our own house, we'd make it look better," or "If I were married, I'd fix the place up a bit." That room (or those rooms) are where God placed you now; make the most of them.

And, as Eddie Carswell and Babbie Mason wrote in their beautiful song:

God is too wise to be mistaken.
God is too good to be unkind
So when you don't understand
When you don't see His plan,
When you can't trace His hand—
TRUST HIS HEART.

© 1989 Dayspring Music

---

[1] *Hind's Feet in High Places*, by Hannah Hurnard (Wheaton: Tyndale House, 1975), pages 6, 7.
[2] Harry Ambacher, "Forget it all—And Learn Chinese," adapted.

LIFE'S LESSONS I'M TRYING TO LEARN

ARE YOU LIKE ME?

Do you have a list of all the things you'll do someday? I'll sort all the pictures I've taken over the years; I'll take up a hobby I've always wanted to try; and I'll read all the books on our shelves.

Often, in waiting for the right time, we lose out on the enjoyment, the adventure of now. This constant looking forward to something in the future starts in childhood. "What are you going to be when you grow up?" everyone asks, not remembering that right now, the little one can be a pilot, a fireman, or an engineer—or all of these together, by means of imagination.

When I was in nurses' training, we students draped safety pins around the room indicating the number of months, then weeks, then days left until we graduated. Restlessly, we wanted our studies to be over so we could really begin living. Innocent enough, I suppose, yet I wonder if I made the most of those years, which in retrospect, were among the happiest of my life.

Elisabeth Elliot, who has experienced much in terms of missionary service and living as a single, a widow, and a wife, says:

> "Let not our longing slay the appetite of our living.
> Accept and thank God for what is given, not allowing
> the not-given to spoil it."

Therein lies contentment.

CHAPTER 5

The Importance of Being Friendly

As a teenager growing up in Brooklyn, New York, part of my social life centered around the ice cream parlor (that's "palor" pronounced without the first "r"—as only a New Yorker would do). Whether with a group from church after choir practice, or a bunch of student nurses escaping pharmacology study for a while, the purpose was the same: fun, fellowship, and companionship. The food made very little difference—I don't even like ice cream! The point was to be together. The ice cream parlors that stand out best in my memory were quaint, family-operated places with an aura of the early 1900s. But the name of a modern chain of ice cream shops brings into focus the reason we visited those restaurants. The chain is called Friendly's.

Being friendly is an important key to clearer communication and overall better interpersonal relationships between the married and the non-married members of any organization or missionary team.

Having accepted God's place for you at this time, the challenge comes to live your life to its fullest. Since most people are sociable by nature, the enjoyment of their ministry or employment often relates to the friends they find—or make—along the way. Making or keeping friends is a work in process. Proverbs 18:24 states, *"A man who has friends must himself be friendly."*

The principles in this chapter apply equally to the married and to singles, reinforcing the similarities among Christian workers rather than the differences. So, for this chapter, let's consider these points as appropriate whether you are single or married.

CHOOSING FRIENDS IN THE HOST COUNTRY

As a Christian worker, especially in a foreign country, you have unusual opportunities to practice the art of friendship. As you become more and more acquainted with the local people, your life is enriched by experiences shared with them.

Sometimes, however, you feel the need to be with people more or less of your own nationality. You have your own missionary family, of course, but it is also profitable to cultivate friendships with people serving in other mission and Christian service agencies. Because of differing beliefs and practices, you may not choose to join in their ministry, but you can enjoy pizza and popcorn together. In addition to Christian workers, you may find teachers, students, business people, diplomatic officers, CIDA or Peace Corps personnel, and many more possible associates with whom you might enjoy being friends.

We had a social life even in Chittagong, a place many people dubbed, "The end of the world!" I was invited to receptions for ambassadors, onboard ship parties for Officers of the Fleet, and social gatherings with visiting dignitaries from many places.

One function was the Iowa Farm Association's yearly visit to Bangladesh. USAID staff who hosted the party must have felt their guests from the "Bible Belt" would feel more at home with missionaries than with USAID's usual cocktail-party friends. So for many years Chittagong missionaries received invitations to a gala event with the farmers.

I recall many occasions when four, five, or more English and North American bachelors sat around the table in the house where Lynn and I lived. They were teachers, engineers, or businessmen living overseas on two- or three-year assignments.

For an outgoing individual or couple, there is scope for a wide range of friendships. Those contacts even presented possibilities for evangelism. Most of the young men attended our English-language services. A few accepted Christ as Savior and continue to live for the Lord.

But with all the pleasure these friendships provided, a note of caution is in order for the career missionary. If ministry among expats (as foreigners living abroad are often called) is within the scope of your mission's plans, then regularly interacting with them is essential. Many large cities have international churches where people from an astounding number of countries worship together. If, however, your priority is to establish local churches in the national language, then most of your time and effort needs to be in that direction and contacts with ex-pats kept to pleasant, but less frequent, intervals.

Canadian missionary Isobel Kuhn served among the Lisu people for twenty-seven years. She addressed this issue when she and her husband, John, pioneered in northern Thailand after they were forced to leave China.

"In every civilized city of the Orient," she wrote, "there is a thing called the White Community. The color of your skin elects you to its membership whether you like it or not. In Chiang Mai, Thailand, it will give you a Welcome Party—just merry games and nice refreshments, and get-to-know everybody. For those who are tied down all day to busy schedules (the office desk, the schoolroom, the hospital), it offers relaxation. If you embrace it warmly, you will soon find yourself in a social whirl. It may seem harmless and everybody is so nice you hate to refuse; and you seem petty not to return invitations. Very soon, John and I had to face the question: How much time were we going to spend at parties and social teas?

"Speaking from the mere relaxation side of it, we felt that we OMFers (Overseas Missionary Fellowship) did not need it. None of us were institutional workers and our lives were far from monotonous. We had plenty of variety. But there was another angle to it—the indigenous pattern to which we were pledged. This suggests that relaxation times should be spent with the nationals. Do we need a game of volleyball? Call in the Thai neighbors to take part. The same holds for parties and picnics. Thai friends are always available. This does not mean we never went to a party; it means that this was the pattern to which we felt committed."[1]

Two dangers may arise in friendships you make with those other than your own mission team:

- You can spend time with "outside" people to the exclusion of your own missionary family. This is the group into which God placed you. God chose that housemate, that couple next door, that family to work with, for you at this time. He put you in proximity so you could learn specific lessons from one another. You can thwart this purpose of God by spending too much time in extracurricular activities.
- You can become so involved in keeping up friendships and maintaining a social calendar that you neglect the reason for which you came to serve in this country.

DISTRACTIONS ALONG THE WAY

When I went to Chittagong, my first assignment was to learn Bengali. But after a year, I hadn't made much progress. I didn't have time to; I was having too much fun. Remember those bachelors? Then a mission administrator made a routine visit. He called me for an interview and announced in a gracious but firm tone that I must leave the city of Chittagong and move to Hebron (our jungle station), where I could study without distractions. Although I fumed at the time, I might never have learned the language had

I not made that move into the jungle.

The men were a happy diversion to balance the stresses of language study. But each moved on when his tour of duty was over. God had called me to stay, to work with the people of Bangladesh. In order to do that, it was essential to have a foundation in the language, the customs, and the culture.

Recently, Wally and I met Ned, a single, young, career missionary in full-time language study in the Asian country where he planned to teach Bible. As he showed us around, Ned focused on tourist attractions, the unexpectedly large number of Christian expats he had met, and the delightful coffee shop where he and his friends hung out. He told us he had cut back his hours with a language tutor, and he completely missed a great language-learning opportunity while we were teaching at the Bible college. Since we did not speak the language, we needed interpreters. Ned could have sat in on our classes, hearing familiar Bible concepts first in English, then translated into the language he was studying.

Unlike Ned, you may find yourself called to serve where there is no Western social life, no one with whom to celebrate North American holidays, no one to run to just for the luxury of speaking English. Before you pity yourself, though, look at the gift God has given you—a gift wrapped up in a difficulty. The gift is that no group of Westerners is pressuring you to be more involved with outside activities than you feel you should be. You are forced to forge your closest friendships with nationals. You will have less of a struggle with egocentrism because you will depend on nationals for all the help you need in language and cultural adjustment. Most of all, you will be blessed with the necessity of having only God to run to for comfort, counsel, and love, which will result in a closer relationship with your Savior.

It never helps to compartmentalize Westerners and nationals with statements such as: "These are the people who understand me" versus "I won't ever be able to be real friends with them," or "These are the people I can be myself with" versus "Spending time with them will always be a struggle."

Again, if your ministry is with or for other Westerners, then your time should be invested accordingly. But if you have been called to give your life for the local people, you may have some tough choices to make.

Take Brice and Elizabeth, for example, who were called to work with Muslims in Southeast Asia. There were other expats in their area, and this group actively pursued fellowship and activities that were for Westerners only. These expats were support missionaries—there to serve the missionaries working among tribal people in outlying areas. Brice and Elizabeth, however, wanted to reach Muslims, so their clothing, language study, and ministry focus were different.

To make it even more difficult, Elizabeth found that hanging out with the Western women—who passed around the latest copies of *People* magazine, talked about the latest American TV shows they got on cable TV, and wore Western clothes—was a great temptation to her. The more time she spent with them, the less she was willing to do whatever it took to be appropriate and holy in the eyes of her Muslim friends. She wanted to wear more comfortable and flattering clothes, and to keep up with the latest trends "back home."

For Elizabeth, choosing to spend less time with the expats was not only so she could spend more time with nationals, but also for her own walk with God. As she pulled away from the expats, she struggled because she knew she was going to be considered snobbish. But with much prayer and discussion with her husband, she made the choice to step back significantly.

Other choices followed: She allowed her son to spend more time with national children instead of just Americans; she tried to call a Muslim friend when she felt lonely instead of making an easier, more comfortable choice. God blessed her decision. Not only did God give Brice and Elizabeth good friendships with Muslims, He even provided a national partnership with a church of believers who became a great source of joy and encouragement.

MAKING TIME FOR FRIENDS

Being friendly takes time and effort. It means keeping up correspondence, fitting in visits when friends happen to be in the same place (sometimes that means when in the same continent), and being ready to fit in to another person's equally busy schedule. Or sometimes with local people, it means being willing to drop all the "important" things you were doing to let them know they are more important.

Enjoy wholesome friendships with the many people who cross your path. With international travel being the huge industry it is, you may be surprised at the number of people who show up in the most unlikely places. And as a missionary, you might travel much more than your counterparts at home. Travel to and from the country where you serve, holidays, continuing education, and conferences in your profession are a few of the scores of opportunities to meet new people and renew former acquaintances.

There are few places in the world where a person would be forced to remain alone and friendless. Most people are inherently friendly and respond to warmth as a flower opens to the sun. If being friendly does not come naturally to you, work on it. Start with a smile, or an appropriate greeting. Invite people to your home. Accept invitations that come your way. Put yourself out to be helpful to others. And when you are blessed with friends, cultivate, nurture, and cherish them.

---

[1] Isobel Kuhn, *Ascent to the Tribes* (Chicago: Moody Press, 1956), pages 36–37.

TRUE FRIENDSHIP

Among the items to ask God to supply in your life, a good friend should be high on your list. I met Jim and Marilou Long when they were at their candidate class in 1983. I was on-site for a day or two conducting sessions on the subject of this book. They were trying to discern God's choice of a country. As I watched their interaction and heard how they wanted to serve the Lord, I felt they would do well in Chittagong. I told them so and rejoiced when they were appointed to Bangladesh. They continue to carry out with great expertise their responsibilities in the areas of administration and education.

But beyond admiring Marilou's skills in music and teaching, she is my friend. I have had wonderful evenings in their home (Jim is a cook par excellence). I've met the Longs in India, Thailand, and New York City for a little rendezvous. But my chief memories are the many times when just Marilou and I went to a Chinese restaurant in Chittagong—nearly the only eating place available when I lived there. We'd order soup and a snack, and then each of us got out the list we had jotted down of things to discuss. They ranged from personal to work to prayer requests to needed admonitions.

Time oriented as I am, I would start looking at my watch halfway through the soup. One time, Marilou reproached me by saying that it made her feel as though my time with her wasn't important. A true friend puts up with your foibles; a true friend corrects what is wrong. A true friend loves at all times.

CHAPTER 6

The Ultimate Friendship

At age 22, when Beth became a missionary, she didn't mind being single. In fact, she enjoyed being able to focus more time on ministry, having a more flexible schedule (staying up till 3 a.m. writing a curriculum if she wanted), and investing herself more in encouraging others.

In transition after four years in missions, Beth's administrator's wife asked her to come to ABWE Headquarters for a two-day conference. What Beth wasn't told was that a certain man named Dave would be there, and her administrator's wife wanted her to meet him. Had Beth known, she would have avoided him like the plague—she hated being set up!

Beth met Dave. Dave liked Beth. A week after the conference he called her. Two weeks later he flew to visit her. They had spent fewer than four days together when Beth flew to Africa. They traded e-mails almost every day, and nine months later Beth headed home to the US. They were engaged within three weeks and married three months after that.

Obviously this isn't the whole story, so we interviewed Dave and Beth for more information.

Dave, what influenced your decision to marry Beth?

I had been asking the Lord's will concerning this for years. Humanly speaking, I wanted a wife. I didn't want to go into overseas missions single. It was scary, and I felt I'd be incomplete in my life and ministry. I wanted someone who truly desired to please God, not just talk the talk.

Practically speaking, I needed a helpmate. The Sunday school kids in my church were praying for a wife who could cook so I wouldn't starve!

After I met Beth, I couldn't get her out of my mind. I prayed a lot for God's direction. Unfortunately, He wrote nothing in the sky. I had knots in my stomach when I called her. But I wanted to spend time with her to see if we enjoyed one another's company, to see her heart for God and her perspective on life.

During the brief time we had together, I learned about those things. I also sensed a peace from God. I asked for and listened to counsel from my parents and other godly people. When I was sure it was God's will for us to be together, I asked Beth to seek God's will about spending the rest of her life with me (in unspeakable bliss, of course).

Beth, how did you know God wanted you to marry Dave?

The unspeakable bliss, of course! But, seriously, this was one of the biggest decisions of my life, and I was scared of making the wrong choice. I asked Dave for one month. We were hardly in contact at all during that month I spent seeking God's will for my future. Could we serve God more effectively together than separately? Would I better serve the Lord single? What was God's will for me? I looked up every verse I could find on marriage, being a wife, and having a family. By the end of the month, I had my answer. God wanted me to serve by Dave's side.

Dave, what are the advantages and disadvantages of serving God as a single?

As Paul said, I had the freedom to devote myself to serving God. I could get involved in whatever ministries I had time for. As a married man, I am very busy, and because of responsibilities to my family, I have less time for ministry.

Beth, what challenges did you face?

By accepting God's choice of marriage for me, I felt less significant as a wife and mom than I used to as a "full-time" missionary. I had to learn to be content to serve my family first before doing the "big" things, to train my own child instead of a larger number of international children, and to have less connection with national single women.

But there were challenges to being single, as well, such as loneliness, not having a husband to run to, or to fix things for you, or to bounce ideas off of.

Dave, what are some difficulties for men in ministry?

The struggle of being content while single waxed and waned. Some nights I would cry out to God, longing for someone to share my life with. I wanted someone who would not come in and then go out of my life; I wanted someone who cared about me and would make a home with me.

When I was blessed with a wife, most of those longings were met. Marriage, however, involves selfless service if it is to honor God.

As a single, you don't get the positives of family life, but neither do you have the work and frustration. I am a happily married man, but there are times when I wish for freedom to give myself wholly to ministry.

Beth, what about serving God single, then married?

Some of my college friends thought God might want them in missions, but they were afraid it might mean they would never marry. That never made sense to me. It's just as easy for God to have two people meet in the jungles of Africa as in a city in North America. If God has someone planned for you, you'd better be where He wants you to be so you don't miss it!

I will always be glad God allowed me to be a single missionary for five years. I love it that God called *me* into missions, not just my husband, and that He has let me serve Him in so many different ways.

But, there are great things about being married, too. My relationship with my husband shows me a reflection of Christ and His church. My husband feels more effective because of my help, and now as a wife and mother I can interact better with families.

Anything else you'd like to add?

Beth: I've learned that my joy, peace, and effectiveness are not based on whether I serve single or married. Contentment and joy are available just as much in one state as the other, because they come from God, not from circumstances. Whatever God's will is for you at this time in your life really is best.

Dave: God works all things for the good of those who love Him, to conform them to the image of Jesus Christ. His desire is for us to glorify Him, to relish the life He has given us today, and to trust Him for tomorrow.

HOPE DEFERRED

As Beth mentioned, the fear of never marrying keeps many singles from career missions or, if they do go, keeps them from being happy. I have received many letters from women who wrote in this vein:

> "Perhaps you would tell me how you find it as a single woman in your circumstances. What do you do about the human, natural cravings for love, affection, and attention? I hope you don't mind my asking these personal questions I am coping with. I am 26 and single, and I crave tender, loving care."

In answering her, I wrote:

> "There are no easy, pat answers. I can only share what I have found to be helpful. My underlying conscious feeling

is that God loves me and knows what is best for me. This is more than just a pretty phrase. I have seen it work so many times. I get an idea in my head and scheme, and struggle, and the whole thing flops, but when I turn it over to the Lord, He has a way of working things out. The only way I have found to have joy and fulfillment is to concentrate on doing what the Lord wants me to do now, at this moment, in the circumstances in which He has put me. Leave the future entirely in His hands. Don't ask me how it works. I just know that when you stop plotting and designing, God takes over and gives peace and contentment."

For single women, friendships and relationships with guys—or the lack thereof—is an area that can cause much frustration. Some seem able to settle this issue before they arrive in the place where they will serve. It would never even occur to them to suppose they would find opportunities for romance. They recognize and accept that in some cultures it would be inappropriate even to have male friends.

Other singles sincerely believe they have settled the issue until they arrive in the place where they will work. Then the lack of a husband or wife becomes a great need and may take center stage in their thinking. Singles are extremely vulnerable at this point, and some have become involved in unwise relationships or been distracted from the reason they went into Christian service, or even destroyed their own and—by extension—the Lord's work in that area. Satan can have a heyday in such circumstances, as this extreme, but true, example shows:

Pete was an athletic young man who wanted to serve the Lord in a difficult place. He chose a country that was semi-closed to the gospel and began working with street kids. He discovered a soccer ball gave him entrance to almost any area where kids hang out. He kept busy all day but the nights were lonely. Little by little, he began to depend on the housemaid to meet his needs. By the time his colleagues became aware of the situation, she was pregnant. Pete tried to do the honorable thing and marry her, but such marriages were not allowed in that country. Pete returned to his home country in disgrace and left behind a shamed and sorrowful young woman and his child.

Some single missionary women bewail the fact that because they are on the mission field, they don't have dates. Who is to say they would be dating if they were back home? Many women do not date, not because they are thousands of miles from home, but because there is no one suitable among their acquaintances. Please don't feel you have been cheated out of dating and the possibility of marriage because you have chosen to serve the Lord in a foreign land.

Before blaming God and your place of service for your lack of dates or lack of male friends, take a look at your priorities. If every social event must be a romantic encounter and every man a marriage prospect, you are in for trouble. Instead, just enjoy fun and fellowship on a friendship basis.

Sometimes friendships do grow into love when this is in God's plan. From time to time, two people from very different parts of their homeland or from two different countries meet in yet a third country. A romance blossoms and leads to marriage.

This is an area where "slow and steady" is a good motto. If you meet someone in whom you are interested (assuming, of course, this person is a believer and the feeling is mutually shared), pray much and accept good counsel from your fellow Christian workers. Communicate with your family, your pastor and home church, and leaders in your organization. Be very sure before you take the permanent step of marriage.

With the right man or woman, however, the missionary can have a happy and fulfilling life no matter where he or she settles, whether overseas or in one or the other's homeland. Take Jean for example: She once told me that she prayed God would keep her committed to her ministry and the team she lived and worked with, yet flexible enough to marry if that was in His will. As it turned out, that was God's plan. After eight profitable years in hospital service, God led her to become a pastor's wife.

BETWEEN THE LINES

Teasing: Bitter or Sweet?

Closely tied to the matter of letting friendships follow their natural course is the problem of teasing. Teasing is part of family life, but sometimes contains a barb. I have found husbands guiltier of this than their wives. Some men seem to need to say something about a single woman's getting married—or not. Be careful about flippant remarks. You don't know what the single you are talking to has gone through. You don't know the person or proposal she turned down so she could be where she is right now. You don't know if she is currently corresponding, weighing the issue: Shall I stay here and do this work, or shall I go home and marry him? Remarks spoken in jest can cause a lot of hurt.

Sometimes married couples nip a friendship in the bud by reading more into it than is there. I remember a young widower who visited our hospital in Bangladesh. Among the missionary staff was a teacher he had met once before. He invited her to play tennis. Before the first set was finished, all the married matchmakers had them engaged. But the man soon went on to Hong Kong and later married a woman in missionary service there.

Another situation involved Alyson, a lovely young missionary from New Zealand studying in language school in India. It was common knowledge that a young man—also from New Zealand—would soon join the class. The couples assumed, "John is coming. Your husband is on his way." Alyson built wonderful dreams. When John arrived, he never once looked at Alyson in a romantic way. Instead, he married a Canadian woman ten years older than he. That couple lived a happy, useful life of service for the Lord. Alyson returned to New Zealand brokenhearted. Classmates made too much of the coincidence of people from the same country. They teased Alyson into believing something that wasn't to be. Teasing can be fun, but be sure it doesn't hurt anyone.

CROSS-CULTURAL MARRIAGES

Marriage may indeed be in God's plan for you, but be very sure before you make that decision, especially if the person is from a country or culture other than your own. Even if the person is of the same race and speaks basically the same language, there may be too many adjustments to bridge the two cultures. For instance, I used to get annoyed when one of my English friends wanted to know, "What time do we feed?" To me, "feed" is something animals do, not people! Or, when I had made a beautiful apple pie and Keith asked where the custard sauce was "to wash it down with." These are surmountable obstacles, of course, but don't assume that because you are there and he or she is there, God has brought you together for anything more than friendship.

Marrying a national of the country to which you have gone to serve is also a possibility for a single missionary. Local women may be beautiful and well trained to be good wives and mothers. Local men may be charming and seem very Westernized.

Some cross-cultural marriages work out well. On the other hand, sometimes an unscrupulous man takes a missionary bride as his ticket to life in a new country.

In less dramatic cases, the problems of straddling two cultures can outweigh the joys of marriage. This may show in a strong nationalistic pull or cultural rules and taboos that require giving up your own customs and culture. For example, Indian men tend to spend their social life with other men rather than with their wives. Indian women most often sleep with their children and feed them by hand until they are well into the elementary grades.

One problem area in some cross-cultural marriages is privacy—a trait Westerners highly cherish, but something often not understood by Easterners. Lydia was a missionary nurse from Australia. After a few years of service, she felt the only way she could get close to the local people was to marry one. Lydia asked various missionaries to help her in this quest for a local husband. Their advice was to think this through again. But seeing her determination, they found a man of a similar age who was working in a hospital. The two married. Lydia's father-in-law accompanied them on their honeymoon. From the moment they set up housekeeping, they were never alone. Sisters, brothers, cousins, aunts—relatives of all ages came to visit and often stayed weeks or months. Lydia was expected to cook, clean, and do the laundry for all these guests. This greatly reduced the medical missionary work they had hoped to do together. The continual lack of privacy also adversely affected their marriage.

In the past thirteen years, fourteen ABWE missionaries have married nationals. Two of these are men whose wives joined the mission and the couples continue to work with ABWE. Three women who married national men remain in missionary service—two with ABWE—while the remaining nine resigned.

LEAVING YOUR MINISTRY

When missionaries from two different organizations marry, usually the woman joins her husband's agency. In rare cases, they both join a new group.

Leaving your place of service or your organization is a serious decision. Be sure this is what you want. More importantly, be sure this is what God wants for you. Especially after a few years of work, your decision to leave is difficult. It may mean not seeing your adopted country again, never again speaking the language you struggled so hard to learn, never eating the food you've come to appreciate and crave when you are away from it, no longer taking part in decision making for cherished ministries, and losing contact with nationals you love and may have led to the Lord or nurtured spiritually.

If marriage takes you back to your homeland, that means trying to fit into what is often described as the "rat-race." Your years overseas will have changed you, possibly in ways imperceptible to you but obvious to others. After living in the midst of poverty, the waste that is commonplace in the West is shocking. In Bangladesh I knew people genuinely grateful for the slip of used soap from a motel room. Even a shower or tub of clean water seems remarkable after heating and carrying water to get a quarter-inch of water in your tin washtub.

Topics which occupy people's minds often appear trivial. Knowing people who face starvation on one side of the world remains prominent in your mind while you try to be polite with people who agonize over the latest diet fad or go into raptures over their new vehicles.

No decision to marry ought to be taken lightly, but when it involves leaving a fruitful ministry, the choice is that much harder to make. There is the added burden that much of what was your life for the duration of your cross-cultural service will have to stay bottled up inside of you. People quickly tire of hearing about "what we used to do" along the Amazon or in Zaire.

When marriage is in God's plan and left to Him to work out, however, those out-workings can read like a novel. We know: It happened in Bangladesh to Karen Carder and Sam Logan.

I first met Sam in the living room of my mother's home in Pasadena, California. Billed as a "brilliant young scientist," he was a frequent speaker at conferences and rallies on the subject of Science and the Bible. Graduated from Cal Tech with a Ph.D. in Aeronautics and Astronautics at the age of 25, he went on to study medicine. But Sam hadn't come to discuss medicine or science or the Bible. He was about to make his first trip to Asia and wanted all the information he could get. So, sprawled out on the carpet, he looked at my pictures and asked questions.

Sam had been accepted for an overseas work/study program. His first choice was the Memorial Christian Hospital in Malumghat, Bangladesh, but his application was lost in the mail and Sam never heard from Malumghat. Instead, he was heading for the Conservative Baptist Hospital in Kalimantan Barat (formerly Borneo, Indonesia).

I suggested, "Why not stop by and see Malumghat Hospital? When you're traveling that far anyway, a few more miles don't make a lot of difference, and who knows if you will ever get back that way again." The idea made sense. Sam knew Dr. Vic Olsen, the prime mover in establishing the hospital.

I met Sam next in my apartment in Chittagong, Bangladesh. A group went to the airport to meet him at the scheduled time, but he wasn't on the plane. I had barely arrived home, however, when in he walked. Sam's flight had been changed, but armed with the sketchy map I had drawn in California, he found us.

He was expected at our hospital (a sixty-five-mile, three-hour bumpy ride away), but they were in the midst of an infectious

hepatitis siege. Before he could go to Malumghat, he would have
to have a gamma globulin shot. So my "Welcome to Bangladesh,
Sam" was with two 5-cc syringes.

As he was leaving for the hospital, he asked if I knew a woman
doctor named Karin Ahlin. She was working in Bangladesh, and
her church asked Sam to look her up. I assured him I knew her and
would have her address for him when he returned. Then I added
rather glibly, "But if it's Karens you are looking for, we have a nice
one at Malumghat."

Karen Carder, R.N., first came to Bangladesh on a missions'
trip with her church. She wanted a taste of life on the mission field
with a view to future involvement. Karen continues the story:

"On arrival, I was hit with overwhelming culture shock: the
hordes of people, the dirt, poverty, and general lack of comfort.
We were immediately taken to Kaptai Lake, where our pastor was
the speaker at the missionaries' Spiritual Life Conference. Kaptai
had been described as a resort. It was like a bad joke. But since no
one else seemed to mind the appalling conditions, I felt very much
alone in my distress.

"Ironically, the single women stayed in what was dubbed the
'Honeymoon Cottage.' After a gab session, the others went to
sleep. I, however, stayed up nearly all night, while the Lord dealt
with the inner rooms of my heart, with things that were keeping
me from serving Him in Bangladesh. Those included cleanliness
and leaving my comfortable surroundings. Although I had previously dedicated my life to the Lord, that night marked a new love
for the Lord and a desire to serve Him wherever He would
choose."

By the next year, Karen was at Malumghat engrossed in Bengali
language study. She was contented and looking forward to plunging
full time into the hospital's medical/surgical evangelistic program.

Sam arrived at Malumghat just as the weekly medical committee meeting was finishing. He was introduced all around, and was trying to place everyone, when he saw a young woman through the curtains between the living room and the verandah. Karen had fallen victim to hepatitis and was not yet well enough to attend the meeting. Hearing the meeting breaking up, Karen went out to the living room to have a word with her doctor. In those few minutes, Sam and Karen had their first glimpses of each other. Almost immediately, Sam was whisked off to dinner and Karen returned to her room.

Back in North America many friends had suggested this or that young woman as God's choice for him. Sam held them at bay, replying, "When I find the right one, I'll know it." That Tuesday afternoon, Sam knew! He found Karen. But he only had five days, and ostensibly he had come to see the hospital.

Sam asked his evening hostess if it were permissible to visit patients with hepatitis. (They innocently assumed he wished to see Dr. Olsen's wife, Joan, who also had the disease.) Sam made the courtesy call but then explained that Joan was not the patient he had in mind. Eventually, arrangements were made for Sam to meet Karen, but the time got mixed up and Sam walked in the wrong door, thereby catching Karen in her grubbies at the ironing board. As word of Sam's growing interest spread, everyone became very helpful—too helpful! Missionary kids suddenly had urgent business that kept them going back and forth in front of the verandah of the nurses' home where Karen lived.

In spite of well-meaning missionary friends and cultural taboos, they did find time to be together. As they talked, they found common interests and mutual aspirations. Not many knew they had come to an "understanding" during those days. They corresponded voluminously during Sam's time in Indonesia, and by then no one was surprised when Karen announced she was returning to the US to marry Sam Logan.

Over the years, they have served short-term many times in
Bangladesh and other medical ministries. One of their four sons
and his wife are now career missionaries. If marriage is in God's
plan for you, God will work out the details.

THE MAN OR THE MARRIAGE?

By the time Wally returned from Durban, South Africa,
in April 1996, he had phoned and we had corresponded
enough that I felt sure he was going to ask me to marry him.
He had met my family, and decision time was near.

The perfect confidante was right where I was, at our mission headquarters, in the person of Eleanor Walsh. Jay and
Eleanor Walsh were among the first people I met when I
landed in Chittagong in 1963. For a while they lived in the
apartment under mine. Eleanor taught me much in those
early days: How to can meat and chicken at a time when we
were given too much, and to use what God gives you. I
hoarded cans or packets of food for special occasions only to
find the tins had bulged dangerously and packaged items
tasted like sawdust. Eleanor's philosophy was: "You can't
expect God to give you any more until you have used what
He's already given you." After three decades in Bangladesh,
the Walshes were asked to oversee volunteers building new
mission facilities in Harrisburg.

So on that Easter weekend in 1996, it was Eleanor I talked
to. She had seen the beginnings of this romance, so she wasn't
surprised when I said what I wanted to talk about. She asked

an insightful question: "Do you love Wally and want to marry him, or are you in love with the idea of getting married?" I've reflected on that question from time to time when I'm frustrated with something Wally did or did not do. *Why doesn't he just do as I say,* I've thought. Then I realize, uh-uh, that's not the way it works. I willingly choose to love, honor, and obey; to work through frustrations, with God's help; and to build and maintain "The Ultimate Friendship" with Wally.

CHAPTER 7

I'm the Only One Really Busy Around Here

My fortune cookie read: "God must like time; He made a lot of it." So true, but time, schedules, and busyness can cause disharmony among married and non-married colleagues. They can be major factors in interpersonal and intercultural relationships.

BETWEEN THE LINES

East Is East; West Is West

To a person from the East, one mark of spirituality is a calm and quiet way of life. A spiritual man knows how to wait, indefinitely if need be. He doesn't run in all directions like a rubber band ready to snap. The Western concept of work-work-work repels most Asians. And what other continent besides North America has a mountain called *Rushmore?*

What is soul-nourishing calm to the Easterner comes across to the Westerner as laziness. Perhaps Rudyard Kipling summed it up best in his classic:

"Now it is not wise for the Christian's health
    to hustle the Aryan brown,
For the Christian riles, and the Aryan smiles,
    and it wears the Christian down;

And the end of the fight is a tombstone white
with the name of the late deceased,
And an epitaph drear: A fool lies here
who tried to hustle the East."[1]

It is not only in dealing with other cultures that busyness problems arise. We all get that "deer-in-the-headlights" look as we breathlessly gasp, "I'll never get it all done.

Frequently I catch myself working up to a full-blown case of "busyitis." In those times I have been helped by repeating, almost as a prayer, John Greenleaf Whittier's words:

Drop Thy still dews of quietness
Till all our strivings cease.
Take from our souls the strain and stress
And let our ordered lives confess
The beauty of Thy peace.

Problems with colleagues may arise because we tend to feel no one else can possibly have as much to do as I do. Nobody can be as busy as I am.

Busyness is a state of mind that often has little or nothing to do with responsibilities. It is quite possible to be busy doing nothing of lasting value. A missionary often sets his own schedule with no time clock to punch. Sometimes the day that loomed so full of opportunities is frittered away on time-consuming trivia. In many locations, each missionary's work is a law unto itself. No one is responsible to coordinate the efforts and check the outcomes. Usually there are no concerned pastors (or ones brave enough) either on the mission field or during home ministry to ask why you didn't attend the special prayer meeting or engage in a particular church outreach. Yes, there are emails, reports, and prayer letters to supporters, but these can be fudged or shrouded in foggy words such as: "The Lord is really blessing." Such a statement doesn't tell if there has been a revival in the church, a new baby born, or if the chickens are laying well.

In recent years, more and more churches are asking, "Who keeps track of the missionaries?" Some churches send periodic questionnaires, but often these lack focus. Rather than being concerned about workloads, goals, and problems of work priorities, they ask spiritualized questions: "How many souls did you lead to the Lord last month?" not realizing that preparing the soil, planting the seed, and nurturing the new plants are the difficult, time-consuming tasks. Or the questionnaire may reflect a theological debate in North America and be designed to check the missionary's position. Each of these may come with the veiled threat of support being dropped if the missionary does not adhere to the particular point of view of the people asking the questions.

Such questionnaires don't help the missionary in setting personal and work objectives. Rather, they add to the rationalization: "I can't get anything done around here for all the paperwork I have to do."

Please excuse me if this comes across as if I'm questioning your diligence in the work you are doing. You may say you work from dawn to dark and barely have time to greet your family or housemates, read a book, or have some fun. I wonder, however, about all that activity and if you really need to carry so much responsibility alone.

Most countries, especially developing countries, are strongly nationalistic. They want the job opportunities, including the top positions, for their own people, not for a series of expatriates who rotate the posts among themselves.

TRAINING YOUR SUCCESSOR

The most important work any missionary, single or married, can do is to train someone else to do his job.

II Timothy 2:2 implies that you teach people who are of a caliber to teach others: *"The things that you have heard from me among many witnesses, commit these to faithful men (and women) who will be able to teach others also."*

No matter what professional label we wear, no matter what appears on our job description, we need to be involved in training others. ABWE's third president, Dr. Wendell Kempton, often quoted this statement: "Success without a successor is failure." Those words were my motto as I watched God work beyond my wildest imagination in the Literature Division in Bangladesh. I founded and guided this publishing center for many years, then turned it over to a national board and local director. When Wally and I attended the twenty-fifth anniversary of the Literature Division, I had one fear. The Bangladesh pattern for celebrations is that the "Chief Guests" sit on a raised dais wearing a lei of fragrant blooms. I didn't want to sit in an elevated position, and I sneeze when I get too close to marigolds. But my fears were unfounded. As we entered the auditorium, Tarun Rangsa, the Literature Division manager, escorted us to seats in the front row and said, "We will not have chief guests; we want all the glory to go to God." Hallelujah!

Often we find it easier to do the work ourselves rather than show someone else how to do it. Perhaps it is a bit humbling to think someone might be able to do the job as well as we do—or even better. Maybe we are afraid to allow change and innovation. If we are to build anything of lasting value, we must pass the baton to others. They must make their mistakes—as we have. They must be encouraged to take over. God explained this to Moses just before he finished his work: *"Commission Joshua, encourage him and strengthen him, for he shall go over before this people, and he shall cause them to inherit the land"* (Deuteronomy 3:28).

THE LORD JESUS' TIME MANAGEMENT

Encouraging, training, and strengthening takes time. And that is just what we feel we don't have. Some people write a "To Do" list and enjoy striking off each item as it is finished. Others become frustrated seeing the long list of items still undone. I often lose the list.

I have read many books on time management, as I am sure you have. One list of fifteen ways to be more productive left me tired before I had finished reading. It included rules such as:

- Use your spare time to get several things done at once.
- Crack the whip over yourself. Require production of yourself.
- Make yourself work. Don't let your moods control your work.

At a time when many of my colleagues and I felt particularly worn out, Dr. Russ Ebersole, missionary to the Philippines, and ABWE administrator, gave the finest biblical principles on "The Lord's Use of Time" I have ever read or heard.

BETWEEN THE LINES

The Lord's Use of Time

1. **Our Lord was conscious His Father had a plan for His life** (John 5:30; John 6:38; Hebrews 10:7; John 17:4).

   Are you sure you are obeying God's will for you today?

2. **To Our Lord, it was imperative that He follow the Father's will** (John 9:4; John 4:34).

   We, too, have only a limited time in which to do the Father's will. Will we be able to say, like Paul, "I have finished my course"?

3. **Our Lord knew there was adequate time to fulfill the Father's will in His life.**

Jesus often spoke of "my hour." That didn't just apply to climactic experiences but to every hour of His life (John 2:4; 7:3; 8:20; 12:22; 12:23; 13:1; 17:1).

Amy Carmichael wrote, "There are enough hours in every day to do God's will for us in that day."

4. **Our Lord lived an ordered life.**

Even though He had many responsibilities, He was not pressured by crises. Consider Jesus' actions concerning his friend Lazarus in John 11:6. Jesus did not rush away from what He was doing at the time, because He knew what He would do later would be better for all concerned.

General Dwight D. Eisenhower once said, "Urgent matters are seldom important; important matters are seldom urgent."

5. **Our Lord had time for people. His was not an attitude of,** *"Come back some other time, I'm busy now"* (Mark 10:13; Mark 5:35; Philippians 2:20).

Interruptions did not disturb the Lord's peace because He knew God had planned those. Rather than being upset by people who throw your plans out of line, thank God people come to see you. Allow time for interruptions: for that knock on the door from someone who needs you, and especially for the little voice that says, "Mommy, read me a story" or "Daddy, come play with me."

6. **Our Lord had His priorities straight.**

In Mark 1:37–38 we read, *"Everyone is looking for you!"* But Jesus said, *"Let us go into the next towns, that I may preach there, also, because for this purpose I have come."* Jesus didn't get sidetracked from God's will.

What are our priorities in life and ministry? Are we doing

everything to see that these are being carried out? Here are valuable questions:

- What am I doing now that really doesn't need to be done? (We can be extremely busy doing things God never intended us to do at all.)
- What am I doing now that someone else could or should do? (We need to learn to delegate jobs.)
- Is what I am doing wasting my own or another person's time?

7. **Our Lord took time to be alone with His Father.**

It may be that the reason we are doing what we should not be doing, and not doing what we should be doing, is because we don't take the time to find out what God has scheduled. The person who spends time with the Lord, planning his day, will be more effective (Psalm 46:10; Isaiah 30:15).

THE PRIORITY OF PRAYER

The problem of busyness, of living in harmony with our single and married colleagues, can be solved only when a person makes the effort to spend time with his heavenly Father. There will be those who feel it should not be necessary to write such words to missionaries, prospective missionaries, and other Christian workers. But I know firsthand the difficulties of establishing and maintaining a regular program of Bible study and prayer. I can think of many things that simply have to be done during the time I've set aside for this. For a while I used to fool myself by saying, "Lord, I'm really more of the 'do-er' type. Let me work while somebody else sits and prays, okay?" Then I read—really read—this great missionary verse: *"Pray the Lord of the harvest to send out laborers into His harvest"* (Luke 10:2). To whom was the Lord speaking? To the seventy disciples He was sending out to preach, teach, and heal. Missionaries themselves must be "pray-ers" as well as "do-ers."

I still would not consider myself a "prayer warrior," although I envy and commend those who are. I find myself more in the pattern shown in Deuteronomy 6:7, talking and thinking about God *"as you walk by the way."* When I watch the news, read of dire situations, or hear the blare of a siren, I pray right then for those involved. I try to maintain an attitude of prayer; as I hear of an urgent need or read an emergency e-mail, I lift the people mentioned up to the Lord right away.

Maintaining a quality *Quiet Time*—as the Intervarsity devotional booklet was called—cannot be stressed enough. Many people seem to have lost this habit and speak of praying while doing other things such as exercising, jogging, or driving to work. Those are excellent additional times to pray, but nothing can replace uninterrupted time with the God of the universe. Think of it: Our heavenly Father wants us to come into His presence and worship and fellowship with Him!

PRACTICAL POINTERS

The spiritual side of managing time, however, is not isolated from practical life. Sometimes a reminder of simple courtesy and common sense is in order.

 To those who are married: Don't assume that because a person is unmarried, he or she will have more time available. That is generally not true. In addition to the hours spent at regular tasks in a hospital, school, or office, the unmarried person still has to manage the house, arrange for meals, entertain company, take care of clothes, prepare lessons, and tend to correspondence. These are ordinary, everyday things that have to be done whether a person is married or single. In a family, these tasks can be shared, dividing the load among more people, whereas the single person might have to handle everything alone. Don't pile work on the singles because you assume they have nothing else to do.

 To the singles: Be patient with your married colleagues. When they don't come to work, don't finish the report you need, or can't teach the class, consider that perhaps they were up all night with a sick baby. Perhaps an older child needs them at home. Remember their priorities. In the case of a wife, she is responsible first to God, then to her husband; anything else comes farther down the line.

Sometimes the unmarried forget that the married women's home is her top priority. That home can be a godly role model in a non-Christian culture. And how will new believers from a non-Christian background learn to raise their children for God unless they see that lived out before them?

Some married women, however, feel that being "keepers of the home" is all that is required of them. But being a good wife and mother is a biblical requirement for *all* Christian wives. For those who have dedicated their lives to be missionaries, that is basic. The woman whom God has called into Christian service usually will want to—and most often will be expected to—be involved in ministry, as well. What she is able to do at various stages of life will change over the years and vary with her training and the ages of her children.

All missionaries and other Christian workers will want to have a clear conscience that they are spending their time in a responsible way before those to whom they are accountable: God, their organization, and their supporters.

There are some things you might have done in your homeland that you just won't have time to do in your place of service. I've observed, for instance, that missionary kids remember going visiting with Mommy much more than whether the cookies were iced or not. They will look back on times when the whole family distributed leaflets advertising special meetings much more than remembering whether or not the house was always spotless.

PASSING THE VISION ON TO MKs

Both married and singles working with MKs should encourage children to have a part in the work. For a few years when I was a child, my father was the Canadian director of the Leprosy Mission. The office was short-staffed, and often my brother, Bruce, and I were conscripted to fold letters, stuff envelopes, and affix stamps. I don't remember it being a hardship. Rather, we felt we were needed.

Some mothers feel they must make everything exactly as it would have been back home or they will rob their family of its heritage. Actually, most children who grew up overseas have a far greater hankering for the national dishes than they do for Grandma's apple pie. There may be some traditions you would have kept up had you stayed at home, but you didn't stay there. You are among those who have heard God's call to serve Him cross-culturally.

I confess I am a traditionalist. I like things to be as they have been "world without end." But there is no use in frustrating yourself and others because everything can't be done exactly as it was back home.

Some feel that to maintain proper health, they must eat imported food and prepare meals identical to those they ate in their homeland. That isn't true. You can study local products and learn to substitute guavas for apples, pumpkin for yellow vegetables, cut-up chapatis for tortilla chips, and many other creative alternatives.

Experiment with local fruits and vegetables. You and your kids may come to like them—at least as well as you like any vegetables. In Bangladesh, a long, green, soft, rather tasteless vegetable graces our tables from May to November every year. We call it by its local name, *chichinga*. That sounds more appealing than snake gourd, which I understand is its English name. But whatever the adults may think of it, ten-year-old Doug, upon learning it wasn't an everyday dish in Michigan where they would spend their furlough ministry, said, "Mom, they don't have *chichinga* in America. Could we take a barrel of it home with us?"

In preparing a meal for visiting missionaries from Hong Kong, an American hostess was excited to give the children the treat of fresh, whole milk. After trying this drink, which was much richer than she was accustomed to, the youngest child whispered, "Mummy, do you think she has any *powdered* milk?"

BETWEEN THE LINES

Busy Here and There

Busy-busy-busy! Life whirls about us. We have so much to do and so little time to do it. We seem to lose focus and become like the man we read about in 1 Kings 20:40. This is a story from the time of King Ahab, when a prophet was assigned to guard a captive. Unfortunately, we read that the prophet tells the King, "While your servant was busy here and there, the man disappeared." The guard blew it because he was too busy to do the one thing he was supposed to do. Often, as Christian workers, we, too, are so busy "here and there" that we miss carrying out the commission given to us by our Lord.

Some people in Christian service put out tremendous volumes of work, but work is their whole life. They are workaholics, and never (or seldom) take time off for relaxation and reflection.

Since I tend to fall into this category, I am indebted to my mother, Jeanette Lockerbie Johnston, for the insights in the following devotional, written for homemakers, but applicable to us all:

> We can learn from the Arab who just sat down one day. When asked what he was doing, he replied, "I'm letting my soul catch up with my body." We need times to do nothing. We will return to our duties much the better for having had some time off. The chance to walk away from pressure for even a short time helps us gain a fresh perspective. It can restore our calm and revitalize us to be more effective. The length of the free time is not so important as the fact of it. It's something to look forward to, to break the monotony or alleviate the grind. And it's important that we feel no guilt, no "policeman over our shoulder" sense of wrongdoing for having taken a break.
>
> The Bible speaks of "pleasures for evermore" in the future (Psalm 16:11). So, we can be sure the Lord is not against either leisure or pleasure in moderation while we are here on earth.[2]

---

[1] Rudyard Kipling, "The Naulakha" from *Songs From the Book* (New York Doubleday, Doran and Co., 1920), page 110.
[2] Jeanette Lockerbie, *More Salt in My Kitchen* (Chicago: Moody Press, 1980), pages 63, 64.

LIFE'S LESSONS I'M TRYING TO LEARN

COMPROMISE AND COURAGE

When I first wrote this book, I was single; I was a pro at being single. I had been one for many decades.

"Is she the same as she was?" a mutual friend asked one of my closest friends after Wally and I had been married a while. "Of course. I'm still ME," I replied when I heard the question.

Yet, there are differences—most of them related to time. I am a planner. Spontaneousness is good once in a while, but it takes away the fun of organizing and anticipating. Most mornings in that hazy fog of waking up, I plan my day, always with more activities and "to dos" than hours to do them.

Then my "dearly beloved" wakes up and says, "Today let's go to _____, let's visit _____, let's do _____." You can fill in the blanks. They are usually good suggestions, and who could resist that big smile? But his ideas break into my schedule. This is where the fine art of compromise needs to kick in to ensure we both get done what we feel is God's plan for that day.

I've also learned a difference between those from Mars and those from Venus, as the title of John Gray's book declares. The difference is called multi-tasking. I have a number of books, projects, and preparation for speaking engagements running all at once. But when I start to discuss "opportunities" with Wally, his first words are, "Slow down. Tell me one at a time." He says it's a man thing. Are four items really too long a list?

I am fortunate in having a husband who is not threatened by washing dishes, vacuuming, and other housework. When I have a deadline, Wally does more around the house. When he is preparing a sermon or material for a Bible college course, I try to protect his time. It works for us.

Of course, singles can do the same thing: Helping one another is not related to marital status. We all might take for our guide a beautiful verse in Isaiah 41. God has been assuring Israel of His help, then Isaiah 41:6 says, *"Everyone helped his neighbor and said to his brother, 'Be of good courage.'"*

CHAPTER 8

Dependence and Independence

Last Sunday Wally and I ate dinner with a pastor friend in our city. In discussing mutual friends, he mentioned a single woman missionary who serves in Europe. Among other remarks, the pastor said, "She is so independent." He then explained that she had called to ask if his church could send a short-term missions team to assist a new church plant. Those two concepts seemed conflicting to me: being independent and asking for help.

In earlier editions of this book, my illustrations centered on women who were mechanically challenged types like me, who can't get the key to turn in the lock, contend with fold-down car seats, or any of the daily challenges others cope with, seemingly with utmost ease.

I mentioned one married woman who always called an unmarried colleague to stay with her when her husband was away because, as she put it, "I could never stay alone in the house. I'd be too scared." Yet, the unmarried woman she called routinely lives alone.

I related cases where unmarried women immediately call for a male colleague to come to the rescue when something drips or "goes bump in the night."

Many people today, however, pride themselves on being powerful and independent. There's that word again. We would do well to get a definition. My *New Oxford Dictionary* (with CD enclosed) explains "independent" as being "not connected with, and not influenced or affected by others." This seems to be a trait that is neither biblical or desirable.

Rather than being independent, the Christian worker—man or woman, married or single—is entirely dependent:

- upon God
- upon God's people for prayer
- upon his constituency to support him financially
- upon family and friends for encouragement and help
- upon household help to keep things running smoothly
- upon local people to carry out and carry on the work of the Lord

Instead of saying a person is "independent," perhaps "capable" or "competent" might be a better choice of words.

Carol Dennis is an example of capable women. When I first met her in Southern California, she was underneath a school bus making needed repairs. She invited me into her home, where I was to stay during the Missions Conference. Later, while she was away driving the repaired bus on the afternoon home-from-school run, I noticed a basket—or two—of newly washed clothes. With three small kids and their parents in the house, laundry was a never-ending chore. I folded and ironed the clothes. That's a job I enjoy since it leaves the mind free to pray, to think, and to plan. In subsequent years, even after Bruce and Carol went to teach at a missionary school in Brazil, she often dropped me a note or e-mail saying: "Come and see us, the laundry basket is full."

Each person has his or her own areas of skill and expertise. There will be times, however, when indeed a woman needs to— and should—call for help. The following are suggestions that may help interpersonal relationships.

 To those who are single: Whatever you are attempting, try first to do it yourself, or ask another woman to help. Many women know how to change fuses, check the oil, and start the gas barbeque.

There is nothing unfeminine about knowing how to do, and even enjoying, maintenance work.

Get a *Home Mechanics for Dummies* book and follow its advice. After all, the Dummies series advertises that the books "tackle any topic that's complex, confusing, intimidating, or conjures up feelings of anxiety."

When you or your female colleagues can't manage, however, don't be too proud to ask a man for help. And when a man does repair or adjust some mechanical monster, be thankful. Something may be broken at his own home and he may not have found time to fix it, but he feels a responsibility to help a fellow worker. Take his help graciously, but don't abuse his concern by calling him unnecessarily.

When a male colleague goes out of his way to be Mr. Fix-it in your home, it is thoughtful to show your appreciation with some "goodies" from the kitchen, an invitation to a meal, or a goofy gift. Be careful to include his wife in these expressions of thanks. Satan would love to twist helpfulness and gratefulness into occasions for jealousy and suspicion.

To those who are married: It would be good for you, also, to learn to be as self-sufficient as possible. Your husband may frequently be away from home on ministry or business, and you will have to handle household matters and make decisions without his advice. There will be times when you will have to stay home alone. Those are the times to depend on God for safety, rather than needing someone with you all the time.

Often your husband will be engrossed in important work. Rather than interrupting him to help you, learn to work that screwdriver and fix the broken "thingamajig" yourself.

In many countries missionaries have household help. You soon learn that this convenience isn't all it's cracked up to be, as when your laundry turns bright blue from having the clothes all washed together, or when the person doing the dishes breaks the handle off your grandmother's cast-iron frying pan. Usually, however, household helpers are extremely capable. They can get items working again or arrange for a local plumber, electrician, or whatever is needed. Learn to be competent in areas where it is necessary—perhaps for survival. The clinging-vine woman is out of style. And none of you involved in or considering serving cross-culturally is that type of woman anyway. We all know situations where the husband says, "Let's serve the Lord on the mission field." The wife, envisioning snakes, scorpions, and sickness says, "No way!"—and that's the end of the discussion. But you aren't that sort of person or you wouldn't be reading this book. You have enough trust in God and adventure in your soul to at least consider Christian service outside your comfort zone.

It's not just women who need help. Some men are unskilled at checking the oil or clumsy at fixing things. My dad was an excellent preacher. He could also play the piano, cook a simple meal, and take part in a mean game of ice hockey. But give him a hammer? Forget it! Even changing a light bulb called for a round of applause. Men, too, sometimes need to call for help.

PASSING ON THE KNOW-HOW

For parents and teachers, the concept of learning to do things yourself carries one step further into teaching children. Sometimes harassed mothers complain, "There is so much work to do around here. I can't possibly get it all done." Yet they have one, two, three, (or more) helpers. Potential helpers, that is. Children must be taught, motivated, encouraged, or, in extreme cases, made to carry their load of the work around the house.

On mission fields where it is culturally necessary to have household help, it can be doubly hard to train children to carry out household chores. For a few weeks when I was eight or nine, we housed a family of missionaries from India. While the mother underwent medical tests, the father and three children lived with us. Mealtimes were a horror, with one after the other of the children demanding service: "Get me some water." "I need a towel, I've spilled the soup." "Take away this plate." It went on and on. Their father dismissed this by explaining they were used to having household help surrounding the table to meet their needs. To which my mother (after days and days of such provocation) replied, "I am not your servant. There is the kitchen. You may get yourself a drink of water. And now you may help me clear the table."

How much better it is for a child to learn how to take care of his needs in the confines of his own home, whether in North America or South Korea. Working together as a family around the house can be fun. Saturday morning was "clean up the house" time in my home as a child. No one went anywhere or became involved in activities of his own until the house was ready for the Lord's Day and the guests who inevitably arrived. (Dad, of course, was in his study at the church.) Sometimes we sang, played games, or listened to the radio as we worked. Everyone was involved, and then everyone was free to go about his own business.

Picking up toys, putting away clothes, setting the table—there are so many things even tiny children enjoy doing "just like the grown-ups." As children mature, they can be expected to be responsible for certain household duties: cleaning their room, preparing a meal each week, folding and putting away clean clothes. The list will vary with the ages of the children, but no child—boy or girl—should miss out on the obligations and the joys of housekeeping.

Among the early missionaries at Malumghat hospital was a couple, both of whom were doctors. The mother had grown up in India and attended boarding school from the time she was six. She felt she had missed out in not learning to cook and keep house, so she began sending her seven-year-old daughter, Terry, to my house to learn to bake brownies and cookies. We had great fun making and eating our creations. Soon her five-year-old brother, Bruce, said, "I want to learn, too."

Please notice the choice of words throughout this chapter. It talks of being competent, capable, learning to do things. It does not say "learn to be independent." An independent Christian worker is a contradiction of terms, for the Bible says in I Corinthians 3:9: *"We are fellow workers with God."*

I often wince inwardly when a person, perhaps to cover up obtuseness or just plain rudeness, states, "I guess I'm just too independent."

I often wanted to do more than just wince inwardly when a well-meaning visitor, impressed by what God allowed various single women to accomplish in Bangladesh, would pipe up, "You girls are so independent." That is not a compliment.

Independence is not something to be sought after. We were created to be in relationship with God and with other people.

No one has to be taught to be independent; that is an inborn trait. The toddler says, "I can do it myself," even as he falls and bumps his nose.

BETWEEN THE LINES

Interdependence

I had just written this chapter when the idea was confirmed for me as I read in the *Walk Thru the Bible* studies on the Prophets:

"Medical Science has yet to discover a hand or an eye or a kidney capable of 'going it alone.' Each organ needs the other members of the body to sustain it and nourish it. The only truly independent organs are amputated, dead, and useless. The same holds true in the body of Christ. Each member of the body needs the other members for strength, support, encouragement, and edification. There is a divinely established sense of interdependence."[1]

In acquiring the many skills necessary to be effective Christian workers, one thing we must learn—even if it is hard to learn—is interdependence on God and on one another.

---

[1] Reprinted by kind permission of Walk Through the Bible Ministries.

LIFE'S LESSONS I'M TRYING TO LEARN

PARTNERS TOGETHER

All this talk of interdependence does not negate the Bible's established order for the home. The husband/father is the God-ordained head of the household.

Since 2003 when Wally and I moved from the ABWE office in Harrisburg, we have served as teachers and speakers in sixteen countries. We have observed and interacted with scores of Christian workers. Among the married couples, we have seen wives so meek they rarely are seen or open their mouths. Conversely, we have worked in situations where the wife does most of the talking, answering questions posed to her husband, interrupting conversations, and generally running the show.

Most often, however, we have found godly men and women working as partners, with each one bringing gifts to the equation for the glory of God.

In preparation for revising this book, I wrote to two of my closest missionary friends and colleagues: Lynn Silvernale, with whom I shared a home in Chittagong for more than twenty-five years, and Becky Davey. Becky and I teamed up for our initial support raising and continued going to churches together on subsequent Furlough Ministry visits. In fact, after Wally and I were married, Wally introduced himself to my supporting churches by saying, "I'm the new Becky."

I asked both women to tell me in what ways I have changed since our marriage.

Lynn replied, "It doesn't seem to me you have changed much other than that you do tend to hold back and let Wally take the lead (with your input!) in most situations. This is as it should be."

Becky answered: "You haven't changed a lot, but you display a concern to be submissive in the biblical way to Wally. This has to have been a difficult transition from having been in charge of most activities or decisions with which you were associated. You seem to complement each other well."

I appreciate what they said, but I do struggle in this area. Take this week, for example. We were planning to meet friends, Gerry and Liz, for a day trip. I was full of useless ideas about a place I had never seen when Wally said, "Why don't you just leave it to Gerry and me?"

What a clever idea! Why didn't I think of that?

CHAPTER 9

Take Care of Yourself

For a few years when I was asked to sing at missionary meetings, I chose the hymn "Let Me Burn out for Thee," each line a stirring sentiment of service and devotion for the Lord.

I stopped singing that song because I no longer think God wants us to "burn out." God has given us these bodies, these temples where the Holy Spirit dwells. He expects us to treat them with care and respect, as we would a precious gift. He does not intend that we kill ourselves—literally—by burning the candle at both ends, pushing ahead when we are at the edge of exhaustion, or straining the body's delicate mechanism to the breaking point.

Taking care of our bodies means not only taking care of our health, but also includes taking the time and effort to make sure that we look our best.

PERSONAL HABITS

People may fall into one of two traps in this matter. Some unmarried people may think, *Nobody is looking at me anyway. It doesn't matter how I look.* And some married people may think, *I've already got my spouse. It doesn't matter how I look now.*

It is important never to let yourself go, no matter whether you live in a jungle setting, a remote village, or in a big, impersonal city.

Try to dress as attractively as you can. The question "What shall I wear?" is probably as old as the creation of women. I wonder if

Eve had a choice of leaves? For a woman serving the Lord, the biblical criterion is modesty. She should dress so as to be a credit, not a disgrace, to the Lord. That does not mean her trademark is "missionary frump." An outmoded, unattractive outfit can draw just as much attention as the latest extreme style.

After our first term of service, Lynn, Becky, and I traveled together from Bangladesh to North America. We decided to visit Europe en route. Since we would spend a few days in London, I wrote to a cousin there whom I had not previously met. As bass player in the London Symphony Orchestra, John Honeyman's contacts were more artistic than missionary. He wondered how he would recognize his world-traveling cousin and her friends. At a loss, he consulted people meeting the same flight and was given these clues: "Since they're missionaries coming from a tropical, underdeveloped country, they'll wear long cotton dresses, and their hair will be straggly."

What Cousin John didn't know was that we had shopped in Rome for new suits and shoes, and then visited a hair stylist in Paris. As I recall, I located John in the airport before he picked us out of the crowd.

It's a fact: When you look good, you feel good, and when you feel good, you are able to accomplish far more. Take time to have your hair cut, styled—whatever is necessary. Spend time and thought on your wardrobe. Coordinate outfits. In your place of service, make occasions to dress up. Even if no one is visiting for the evening, the old-fashioned custom of cleaning up for dinner has merit. A warm bath—or a cool shower—clean clothes, neatly styled hair can lift your spirit.

The customs of the country in which you are serving the Lord must be recognized and respected. Occasionally, the presentation of the gospel has been nullified by the clothes of the speaker. In some places no "decent" woman would wear slacks; in other places the pantsuit was the national dress for women long before it was introduced in the West. In some places sleeveless dresses are shocking; in others not only the bare arms but six inches of bare midriff are acceptable. Often, it will be correct to wear the national dress of the country where you are working. Be sure to wear this properly—even the sari, which is just a piece of cloth six yards long, can be worn "in fashion" or not. In wearing national dress, it is wise to check the dress code ahead of time. I remember feeling like a fool at a picnic we had in Bangladesh. I knew we were going to climb to a waterfall, stick our feet in the pool, and eat with our fingers while sitting on the ground, so I wore old clothes. As the nationals piled onto the bus, I was dazzled by the swish of silk and nylon saris and confronted by women and girls who had donned their best. They were going on an outing. They would have their pictures taken beside the beauty spot. "What if your clothes get soiled or torn?" I asked. The answer was, "Then we will always remember that it was on that lovely picnic that it happened."

EAT CORRECTLY AND GET SUFFICIENT REST

Good health often involves controlling your weight. This includes those for whom being either overweight or underweight is a struggle. Even if you live alone, cook balanced meals. Squelch the urge to prop your study materials against the catsup bottle as you gulp down your sandwich.

Eight hours sleep a night remains the optimum even for adults, according to the latest research. I, for one, am always grateful when I am in a culture where taking an afternoon siesta doesn't raise eyebrows. Plan times of recreation, relaxation, and exercise. If you have no place to play tennis or jog, at least you can jump rope or possibly climb stairs.

KEEP YOUR HOUSE CLEAN AND TIDY

Often this is difficult. The rooms may be small and crowded and have no closet space. Or the building may be a museum piece with fourteen-foot-high ceilings and plaster that showers onto your head. Perhaps a lot of people run in and out. Rather than giving up, accept this as a challenge to your interior decorating skills and see how you score on a *Better Homes and Gardens* "before and after" set of pictures.

If at all possible take some treasures and knick-knacks to your field of service. Acquire new souvenirs along the way. Those familiar, lovely objects can be like a breath of fresh air on a sultry day.

I inherited my love of fine English bone china from my mother. In each of the many houses we lived in as I was growing up, there was always a china cabinet, a three-cornered what-not, or a hutch. There, displayed for all to enjoy, were delicate cups and saucers. But we didn't just look at them. We used them regularly. When helping me pack for my first term of service, my mother suggested I choose some I would like to take with me. Thinking practically rather than aesthetically, I said, "Oh, no. They might break. I will have to take plastic dishes."

My mother quietly asked, "And what do you think missionaries used before the invention of plastic?"

So I had china plates and cups and saucers. Yes, a few broke, but so did the plastic dishes. Missionary and local women alike enjoyed using a china cup. "The tea tastes so much better in the Shelley's Dainty Blue," said one dear friend.

HOME, SWEET HOME

Wherever you live, make your house a home. Nearly every woman is innately a homemaker. I once heard a man pray, "May those of us who have homes be good examples to our neighbors," indicating that only families with children can have *real* homes.

I felt like interrupting to say, "Hey, wait a minute. We all have homes and we all need to be examples to our neighbors."

A home with children is indeed a blessed place, but it is no less a home when occupied by a childless couple or unmarried people. Why do homes where single people live get stuck with names such as hostel, residence, or quarters? The place where people live is their *home*, and it is up to the inhabitants to cultivate and develop the heartwarming, cozy atmosphere the word "home" brings to mind.

While vacationing in India I learned of a single woman, well along in years. She worked in an isolated location but had created such an atmosphere of peace that missionaries of all ages and marital status loved to spend a few days of "R&R" with her and bask in her homey influence.

STAY ALERT MENTALLY

We all like to talk about our work and share what we are doing. But don't fall into the trap of being able to talk only about work. It is upsetting and even disgusting to the non-medical person to have a ruptured appendix or a complicated cholecystectomy along with fried chicken for dinner. Throughout the day, remember interesting bits of conversation or anecdotes to share with your spouse or housemates. Conscientiously try to turn off the shop talk when the end of the workday comes.

In a group of young mothers, often the entire conversation is of formula, teething, and potty training. There certainly is a time for such discussions, but don't let that be the only thing you can talk about. Junior will grow up. Then what will you do?

Don't let your mind grow stale. Work a crossword or a SuDoku® puzzle. Be aware of what is going on outside your house and your sphere of work. Listen to the radio or TV. Set FOX News or CNN as your home page or mark them as favorites. Subscribe to the print or online version of news magazines. Try to keep current in the Christian world, also. Subscribing to your denominational and other Christian periodicals will help, even if it takes six months for them to get to you.

Continue, or begin, to receive—in print or electronically—your profession's journal: medicine, nursing, or teaching, to name a few. Subscribe to magazines about your hobby interests: *Field and Stream, Sports Illustrated, Needle and Craft*—whatever you enjoy.

Beyond periodicals, be sure to read good books. Request books when people ask what they can send for Christmas, birthday, or other special occasions. The Customs Department of most countries allows books to arrive duty free. If you are shipping your goods by container, it would make sense to take your personal library. In addition, friends and church groups might be glad to donate books. These will enrich you, and they can be a gold mine for colleagues, nationals who read English, and church and college libraries.

SCHEDULE READING IN YOUR DAY

Don't feel guilty as if you ought to be "doing something" when you are reading. Often, the way to get your own creative juices stirring is to read someone else's writing. You may agree and move forward with your idea, or you may disagree and come up with a whole new approach.

Some of you are saying, "Me—find time to read? You can tell she doesn't have any little kids running around the house. I don't have time to read my Bible, let alone another book!"

It is a fact that you do have time to do what you want to do. Oswald Sanders (1917–1992) was a Christian leader who authored more than forty books on the Christian life. He wrote, "The use of time depends largely on the pressure of the motives."

For a while during my first year in Chittagong, I lived in an apartment above the Walsh family. Jay was engrossed in a pioneer ministry to tribal people. His wife, Eleanor, a nurse, was busy with their seven children (including twins). The oldest child was ten when the youngest was born. Yet Eleanor was probably the best read of our entire team. It was important to her, so she took time to read.

Your reading habits can reap dividends in the lives of your children. Being a good reader and being a good student are often synonymous. A child who sees his parents enjoying good books will more readily pick up a book on his own than will the child in a home where books merely adorn a shelf.

EMOTIONAL HEALTH

This area can make or break a missionary career. Wise was the mission leader who told the candidates to develop or cultivate a sense of humor. Learn to laugh at yourself. For sure, others are laughing with or at you.

BETWEEN THE LINES

Choose Laughter

A missionary wife who was serving in Southeast Asia tells this one on herself:

"A poor elderly lady came to our house selling a brand of fish chips. The chips looked flat and hard, a lot different from the puffy ones I'd eaten, but I chalked that up to my ignorance and bought a bag. I couldn't wait to serve this Asian favorite the next time we had guests. When that day came, I happily poured the hard flat chips into a bowl and took them out to our national friends. However, instead of being impressed at my cultural savvy, they stared at the chips with embarrassment—a bad sign in an indirect society. Finally, my friends told me you have to cook the chips in oil to make them poof out. In the state I had served them, they were like uncooked macaroni—completely inedible! I thought this was hilarious and started laughing, and when I did, my gracious national friends stopped feeling shame for me. They took the hard rocks back to the kitchen and taught me how to cook them.

That experience, which could have turned out to be embarrassing for everybody, ended up being a great friendship builder, and one of my best ice-breaker stories to get nationals to see us as just "real" people. It amazes me how comfortable they become after hearing how I made a fool of myself!"

ABWE's first missionary wife in Bangladesh, Winifred Barnard, told this story. Following a long boat ride, she and her husband climbed up and down hills visiting villages all day. The weather was hot, and by the time they arrived back at their boat Winifred was absolutely exhausted. Her husband found her kneeling by the stream, washing clothes. With tears pouring down her cheeks, she sobbed out her woe, "I don't think the Lord ever intended me to live like this."

As a wise and loving man, her husband refrained from a theological discourse. He brought her a pillow, helped her lie down in the boat, and brewed a cup of tea for her. A short rest restored her to her good humor. She felt foolish about her tears, but at the time and in the midst of exhaustion, the situation had seemed life-shattering.

Mrs. Barnard was not the first to need a cup of tea. British novelist Rudyard Kipling wrote:

We had a kettle; we let it leak;
Our not repairing made it worse.
We haven't had any tea for a week.
The bottom is out of the universe.

Laugh when you can. Cry when you need to. Sometimes—especially for a woman—crying is the best thing you can do. But remember Psalm 30:5, *"Weeping may endure for a night, but joy comes in the morning."*

LIFE'S LESSONS I'M TRYING TO LEARN

WHAT DIFFERENCE DOES IT MAKE?

Wally, for all his good points, has some areas that annoy me. He gives the word "elm" (as in tree) two syllables and says "chorus" in one syllable as though it were "coarse." He can't pronounce Massachusetts at all, and he usually eats up one food group on his plate before starting another. But will those things really matter one-hundred years, or a year, or a minute from now?

HAVE A GOOD LAUGH

Take the day I was finalizing a talk for a women's breakfast. Wally went to buy a few needed items. A while later I was talking on the phone when he dashed through the door. The call was really for him, so I stopped him in his tracks with the phone. Next thing I heard was, "I'll have to call you back. I've left a shopping cart at the check-out counter. I forgot to take my wallet and just ran home to get it."

I couldn't even say, "You've done what?" before he dashed out our apartment door. Later yet, he phoned to tell me to meet him at the front security door with the house keys because in his rush to take his wallet back to the store, he'd left his keys. I opened our door, saw his still dangling house keys in the lock, and—out of habit—locked the door behind me. Then I went down to the lobby, out to the car, and gave him his keys so he could get into the underground parking garage. *Oops!* That's when I realized I did not have my own keys to get back into our apartment building. At lunch, Wally prayed, "Thank you, Lord, for having everything under control, 'cause we sure didn't today."

And then we had a good laugh at each other, and at ourselves.

CHAPTER 10

Discouraged, Down, and Oh, So Lonely

Single or married, man or woman, there may come a day (or month, or year) when you can't laugh it off anymore. A cup of tea won't help; a funny book won't encourage. You are sinking and nobody seems to understand.

Please know, dear child of God, you are not alone. The difficulties you face (or will face) and the pain you feel have been felt before. And you can overcome.

For those going through this now, I wish I could sit with you, cry with you, and pray with you. Since I can't, I'll give what help I can with the prayer that God will show you His love as He carries you through this time. Our heavenly Father says, *"I, the Lord your God, will hold your right hand, saying to you, 'Fear not, I will help you'"* (Isaiah 41:13).

SEVEN PRESSURE POINTS THAT CAN CAUSE EMOTIONAL TURMOIL

These are true examples sent to a young single missionary in emotional turmoil by a woman who served first as a single, then later as a married missionary:

1. Guilt

It's so overwhelming seeing the immense poverty, filthy living conditions, and spiritual oppression. I wanted to rescue all the street kids and beggars who followed me around. I wanted to live on the streets sometimes just to stop feeling so guilty that I had so much more. I hated myself when I realized I could not fix the world's pain.

In North America, most of us are kept as far from pain, evil, and death as possible. Somewhere along the line, however, it enters our lives and knocks us down with a force meant to destroy us and our beliefs. Here's what God taught me: I can't save the world, but He can. He chose to have me born where I was, and others born where they were. I should not hide away because I have more; instead, I should use what God has given me to serve Him and glorify Him. And all the things I cannot do, I must leave in His hands.

Don't try to carry the weight of the world. The burden of it will destroy you. Guilt is not one of the gifts of the spirit. Joy and peace are. Hand over the guilt honestly to God, and accept His joy.

2. Crushed expectations of self

I had all these big dreams of who I was going to be and all the great things I would do for God. When I struggled with issues, I didn't want anyone to know because I thought missionaries weren't supposed to struggle. They were supposed to sound like the people in biographies who always said and did the right thing, who moved mountains and never for a moment wavered.

God taught me that this struggle was less about my desire to serve the Lord and more about my pride. I was so disappointed I wasn't doing great things that I was too busy to do the good God wanted me to do. Spending all day hating yourself is still spending all day on yourself. It does not honor God.

Yes, God does have great plans for you. Yes, He does value you and what He has called you to do is significant. But, remember, it does *not* have to be important in the eyes of the world to be important to God. Obey Him, stay busy with what He wants you to do, and leave the results and the recognition up to Him.

3. Problems with other missionaries

Missionaries are supposed to be the nicest, most godly people in the world, right? Maybe they're supposed to be, but sometimes they aren't. There will be times when missionaries really frustrate and annoy you. That is a shame because it dishonors God. It is understandable, however, considering that each mission team is made up of people who are out of their own culture, away from those with whom they feel comfortable, in a new place with a new language, and have a passion to do what is humanly impossible.

Tension can so easily develop between singles and married couples. Some singles feel they are not understood and their voice doesn't count. Some married couples feel they are misunderstood and that their effort is not appreciated. Communication about thoughts and feelings can minimize misunderstanding and stop resentment before it starts. If someone is having a difficult time, even though he may try to hide it, everyone can tell. It is better to say, "I'm struggling right now." Admit your own humanness.

I hated having to accept that about myself, and I hated having to accept it about others, but the truth is, anytime we put people on a pedestal, they block the view from where it should be—on God. Some days you will desperately need understanding and kindness. Don't forget to extend that to the rest of your team, too.

4. The glamour wears off

In the beginning it's all an adventure. There are pictures to take and stories to send home. You feel excited about learning new things and being part of God's work in the world. But after six months, a year, or two years, the adventures may turn into frustrations; the excitement turns to annoyance; the work isn't coming along as fast as you'd hoped; you are turning out to be less of a hero than you expected; and all you want is to go home to air-conditioning and people who speak English.

This is normal. I repeat, this is totally normal. Don't feel guilty about it, but don't wallow in it either, and don't let Satan use it to get you to quit! The best things you can do when in this state are to pray transparently, keep your mouth closed when you want to complain to others (though you need at least one friend with whom you can be truly open about your struggles), stay busy, and, if possible, spend more time with nationals. Ask God to give you a greater love for them and help you learn more about them.

5. Overextending yourself

There is so much to do and so few people to do it. That's the cry of just about every ministry. Whether you work in a church in North America or on a boat along the Amazon, you'll likely be asked to do more than God has called you to do. Sometimes God wants to stretch you, or teach you a new way He wants to use you. Often though, we say "yes" out of guilt, or just because there isn't anybody else to do it. Watch that trap; it leads to burnout and resentment. My advice would be that anytime you are asked to take on a new task, even something as simple as a one-time speaking engagement, answer, "Give me time to pray about it, please." Do pray and let God direct you. I've noticed that most of the time when I've jumped into something because it seemed urgent, it's something I should have said "no" to. I want to do everything and be superwoman and impress people. But that's self-glorification, and it leads to stressed-out people who are doing tons of stuff for God, but don't have time to really know Him anymore. That's never what God wants.

6. Questioning your faith and God's power

This one is the most frightening. To be painfully honest, the most bizarre and frightening "spiritual" moments I ever had were when I was on the mission field, feeling culture shock, feeling guilty, feeling insignificant, and thinking all my problems were spiritually related. I started thinking God was trying to speak to me through my feelings. I was listening to all kinds of voices that weren't His, and I got to the point where I just wanted to die and be done with it. I woke up every morning feeling desperate and terrified. From those months, I learned this incredibly important truth: Accept *nothing* that does not agree with the Word of God. God does not send any thought or idea that is not found in His Word. So when everything is falling apart, when you're surrounded by dark religions and wondering if what you believe really is the only way, when you are sick and emotionally weak, when you find yourself at the end of all you'd hoped, go to God's Word. Run to it, hang on to it. What He says is real—"the truth will set you free." I learned I cannot trust myself. I cannot trust my emotions. But I can trust my heavenly Father. God is not afraid of your asking questions. He loves you. Whatever you do, when you feel like running, run toward Him, not away.

7. Claustrophobic-feeling rules

I felt the rules for single women were stifling and a bit paranoid. It seemed older missionaries felt responsible for us parentally and made a bunch of rules to make sure nothing ever happened to anybody. By the end of my second year, I had learned the wisdom of most of them, and I discovered several things I had been doing wrong. In almost all non-Western cultures, the rules for women are strict. You're stuck doing whatever the culture or your team decide. In North America, we'd call that oppression; in most of the world, it's just the way it is. If God has called you to where you are, do whatever it takes. To behave appropriately where you are, especially at first, trust the judgment of those who make the rules, especially if they've been there for a long time. Not following cultural norms can harm not only you, but also the Lord's work you've come to do.

Stories often explain things more clearly. Here's one:

> "It sure is good to finally be here," Linda remarked. "It seems forever since we first decided this is where the Lord wants us to serve."

"And we're so glad to have you here," Bev responded.
"You're an answer to our prayers. Oh, by the way, it would
be good if you wore a hat to church tomorrow."

"A hat!" Linda exploded. "I'd look ridiculous in a hat! I
didn't wear a hat when I came here on a missions trip years
ago. I don't even own a hat."

"When you came before, Linda, you were young and single. Now, you're a bit older and you're married. The women
in the church will be shocked if you don't wear one. And
you can easily buy a hat here on our island."

I don't know if the fictitious Linda did or didn't buy that hat,
but the situation is true. Don't let such a simple thing as a hat spoil
your own testimony and, by extension, that of your mission team.

TWO ESPECIALLY DIFFICULT AREAS

In addition to the seven areas mentioned previously, here are two
more. It has been said that the two biggest emotional problems
confronting Christian workers are *discouragement* and *loneliness*.

Discouragement may begin before the career missionary even
arrives in the host country. Setbacks during the years of preparation, financial difficulties, intensive testing, and wearying travel as
you present the ministry to which God has called you—these can
strike down all but those who have declared, "I'll get there, by
God's help, no matter what!"

After the excitement of finally arriving at your place of service,
you face the humbling time of orientation and language study.
Inevitably, someone catches on more quickly than you do, and it
seems as though you'll never learn. This intensifies when local people compare you with other foreigners who learned the language
more quickly or laugh at the way you talk.

As you get into your work, you may have that helpless feeling and start thinking you don't really belong here at all. Everyone else is competent and does the work so easily—and then there's you! Someone assigns you a task and leaves you with a cheery, "Do the best you can." Or, even worse, you aren't doing what you can do well, the things for which you gave up friends and homeland. It is discouraging and easy to seethe with resentment when you seem to be kept from what you planned to do.

When you are discouraged, you are in good company. David, Elijah, and the great apostle Paul, among others, all became discouraged. But they didn't stay in the "Slough of Despond," and you don't have to either.

Discouragements will come. They come to us all, but that is not the time for defeat, despair, or running away. It is the time for practicing a quiet trust in God. Missionary Amy Carmichael wrote, "Things are sure to happen which will drain the heart of human hope, but the hallmark of the true missionary is refusal to be weakened or hardened or soured or made hopeless by disappointment." [1]

Discouragement, disappointment, despair, defeat—all those dreadful "D's" can sap your strength and ruin your ministry. Those moods usually come and go. For some people, however, the main problem is *loneliness,* and it doesn't seem to go away.

BETWEEN THE LINES

Loneliness Defined

Professor Craig Ellison wrote in *Christianity Today*:

"Two basic feelings underlie loneliness. The first is a lack of the sense of belonging. The lonely person is unsure if anyone wants him. The second is the feeling that no one understands. The lonely person has either lost or been unable to form relationships in which he can share concerns with another person who is interested, sympathetic, and accepting.

"The loneliness of not feeling accepted and understood may be experienced by married as well as by single people. Married persons who become too busy in separate spheres of activity, or who do not talk to each other about their feelings for fear of being hurt, or who fail to encourage communication, are likely to experience loneliness."[2]

LONELINESS CAN STRIKE THE CHRISTIAN WORKER IN MANY SETTINGS

I recall the thoughtful married man who lived with his family in a remote jungle setting. Across the compound lived one single lady missionary. "Sure," he said, "we invite her over to dinner, but I always get this feeling in the pit of my stomach when I see her going back into her house alone."

The single or married couple who are the first or only missionaries in an area are completely on their own. They must acquaint themselves with the surroundings, find ways to interact with local people, initiate a program to evangelize these people, and provide social contacts for themselves and their children.

It may sound adventurous to hear about pioneer missionary men who trek to isolated villages, but often it means long hours walking in the sun over rough terrain while blisters the size of golf balls swell on your feet. In an urban setting, it might mean climbing steep stairways in squalid tenements, or pounding the pavement on house-to-house visitation. And—if he is married—while he's on his preaching trip, his wife at home is trying to cope with household help who may resent a woman telling them what to do and with children who may need Dad's steadying discipline.

Donna recalls her situation. "When I was in full-time language study, a tutor came to my apartment every day. My neighbors were Ukrainian and spoke only Russian, so unless I talked to one of my teammates (and they were busy in language study, too), I could go for days without ever saying a word out loud in English. I asked one of my teammates to call me once in a while so we could have a conversation in English. I wanted her to call me so I wouldn't feel like I was bugging her by initiating the phone call every time."

During my first term in Chittagong, I lived alone for several months. I kept busy throughout the week studying Bengali and teaching missionary children in a nursery school. I was often out in the evenings, but Sunday dinner was my Waterloo! Week after week, I had extra salt in my diet as I cried into my solitary Sunday dinner. Perhaps it was more distressing for me because in my family we always invited guests for dinner after the morning service.

Maybe my missionary colleagues had issued a general invitation, "Come to our place whenever you want to." That won't do. Most people don't want to barge in without a specific invitation.

While all men and women can fall prey to loneliness at certain periods of life, there is a specific type of loneliness which attacks those in Christian service. James L. Johnson, missionary to Africa and director of Evangelical Literature Overseas, calls this the "loneliness of the life of faith." In his excellent book *Loneliness Is Not Forever*, he writes,

> "The loneliness of faith comes with the realization that there really can be no one else, except God, who will enter into the journey with you. Yes, some people smile and talk politely, trying to communicate interest and concern. But most seem to remain a long step removed. Sympathetic, yes! But a person in Christian service does not need sympathy; he needs love, interest, even validation.
>
> "Consider missionary Hazel R., who said, 'The worst part of it all is that in twenty years of mission service I never

could get close enough to anyone at home to really call her a friend. People would pray for me, they said, as my name came up on the church's prayer calendar. But they could not pray for me as someone they really knew. Home ministry is often a time of tears for me. I desperately want people to accept me into their inner circles as a person, not a super-human frontier warrior. I wanted to cry with them, laugh with them. I wanted them to do the same with me. Instead, we met, we talked, we passed each other—I did my act, they applauded, and that was that.'"[3]

ORDINARY PEOPLE

Perhaps missionaries themselves are at fault for perpetuating a superman image in letters and reports. If we missionaries aren't willing to share our mistakes, our problems, and our frustrations, people, of course, will assume we are above these common trials of life. And we have no one to blame but ourselves. This is the case whether we are in our home country or abroad. We lose ordinary contact with "Christian workers" who work in the post office or teach in a public school rather than living and working halfway around the world. Maybe by being more open with our support-ers we would dispel the mistaken ideas expressed by a woman who told me, "I'd like to correspond with you, but I live such an ordi-nary life. I don't know what I'd write to a missionary."

Bless your heart, friend. I'm just as interested in the price of coffee these days, and what Mrs. So and So wore to the church wedding as you are. And I need you to tell me things—common, everyday things—just to keep me in touch with life.

Perhaps we have not conveyed our need clearly enough to peo-ple back in the homelands. They don't know how much we need their fellowship in prayer and through the spoken or written word.

We leave sign-up sheets on the table at the rear of the church for those who wish to keep in touch. A number sign up. For reasons of economy, we trim the list down by asking those who are really interested to fill in a card. Still the response may be up in the hundreds. But we don't hear from those people ever—until the next round when we start all over with the sign-up sheet.

Oh, there are exceptions: The little child who says, "I have your picture over my bed. I pray for you every night before I go to sleep." Or the new widow who says, "Jeannie, you've lost a prayer warrior. My husband prayed for you down on his knees every day of his life." Those expressions of love and concern are humbling.

But what about all the rest who are names on a list but you don't know if they are alive or dead? What of churches who regularly send money, but you never know if they have a different pastor or a new program, or if they have moved to a new location.

One of my greatest blessings in my years of service overseas has been regular letters and e-mails from my family including accounts of happenings, news clippings, jokes, cards—things that say, "You're being thought of." In addition to his regular writing, my brother, Bruce, made it his practice whenever business or pleasure took him to a particular organization in New York, my favorite city, to always send me a note on their stationery.

Loneliness strikes from many sources, both on the mission field and at home. The question comes, then: What can you do when loneliness, discouragement, and despair set in?

RECOGNIZE WHAT YOU ARE DEALING WITH

Again quoting from Johnson's book *Loneliness Is Not Forever*:

"Many people cannot distinguish between loneliness, aloneness, and solitude, confusing them all as being detrimental to the human spirit. Solitude, however, is an alone-

ness that is—or can be—creative. Solitude is not loneliness
and need not be a crippler. It need not lead to despair. The
secret of having times of solitude is in understanding that
this is not a process for ill but an opportunity for God to
show Himself as perhaps He cannot do when the landscape
becomes too crowded."[4]

CONSIDER POSSIBLE CAUSES

If you find yourself unexplainably tired and weepy, losing interest
in your work and life around you, check with a doctor. You may
be suffering from a treatable illness. One Christian doctor said, "I
learned long ago that if a person can no longer pray, the problem
might be a thyroid deficiency." Don't berate yourself needlessly.
Go to a doctor, then follow his prescription whether it is for mul-
tivitamins, a daily siesta, or a vacation.

Having consulted with a doctor, it is good to check your spiritual condition. Apathy, dullness, wanting to quit, overwhelming
loneliness—any of these symptoms can mask a broken relationship
with the Lord. Perhaps there is an area of your life that you have
been unwilling to turn over to the Lord; perhaps you are harbor-
ing bitterness toward, or fostering a critical spirit among, your fellow workers. Thank God for the convicting power of the Holy
Spirit working in your life to bring these things to light. Claim the
promise of forgiveness in I John 1:9. Confess the problem and
allow the Great Physician to work in your life.

DO SOMETHING ABOUT IT

When loneliness or depression hit, don't give in; rather, work them
off. "Start a vigorous activity," says psychologist Becky Whetstone
(www.doctorbecky.com). She suggests jogging or pulling weeds.

The activities might have to be adjusted according to the area where you live. Dr. Becky then suggests, "Then do something soothing, like taking a warm bath. This ritual tells the brain to de-stress."

Perhaps more than any other time, when a woman is feeling lonely she needs to guard against the sin of self-pity. "Poor little me! Nobody's ever had it as bad as I do." What a waste of time just to sit and feel sorry for yourself. Get active, especially doing something you enjoy. Again referring to the Walsh family, those of us in the apartment upstairs always knew when Jay was away and Eleanor was lonely. She got out "The Flight of the Bumblebee" and other challenging piano pieces and rattled the keys for all she was worth. That was her way of working off a slump. Find your own method, but do something.

George Bernard Shaw wrote, "The surest way to be miserable is to have the leisure to wonder whether or not you are happy."

TELL SOMEBODY ABOUT IT

If the problems are too heavy for you, don't bottle them all up. Tell the Lord, of course, but also tell a person near you. Perhaps new arrangements can be worked out. Maybe you can move to a new location. Maybe two families can move closer together, or a short-term worker can join you for awhile. Members of your own family might be able to come and visit. With today's easier air travel and excursion fares, having visitors is a viable option. Remember, people are more important than work, no matter how important the work is. If you are lonely or discouraged, ask for help. It is likely that something can be done to help you.

Of course, in the final analysis, the solution to loneliness, discouragement, or any other destructive emotion that drains the soul and weakens the body is a total trust in a loving heavenly Father.

Jim Johnson sums it up perfectly:

> "Taking all the human props away then (if that be the
> case), the man or woman living a life of faith, trusting the
> light he or she has for the journey commissioned by God, is
> never alone. That has become too familiar, of course, but
> the truth still does not wear out with the using. The mystery
> of the presence of God in such a life has kept thousands of
> Christians in the bleakest, darkest, most solitary situations
> on earth. That is why prison cells do not bend them; the
> heat and sun of the jungles and deserts do not crack them;
> wind, fire, and cold do not subdue them; the endless, empty
> prairies or the crowded metropolises of indifferent masses
> have not deterred them; in it all, the man or woman of God
> knows the 'presence' and the 'still, small voice.' In the dark
> hours, there is that promise, *'Lo, I am with you always, even
> to the end of the age'*" (Matthew 28:20.)[5]

[1] Amy Carmichael, *Gold Cord* (Fort Washington, Christian Literature Crusade,
1957), page 75.

[2] Craig Ellison, "The Roots of Bitterness," © *Christianity Today*,
March 10, 1978, used by permission.

[3] James L. Johnson, *Loneliness Is Not Forever* (Chicago: Moody Press, 1979),
pages 90–92.

[4] Ibid, excerpts from pages 177–187.

[5] Ibid.

LIFE'S LESSONS I'M TRYING TO LEARN

DON'T SWEAT THE SMALL STUFF

I can get into such a tizzie when I lose things around the house, or my schedule gets upset, or any number of non-essentials make me too busy.

That's the time to remember an expression we learned in South Africa: "It's not a train smash."

CHAPTER 11

The Challenge of Peaceful Living

Before discussing this vital issue as it relates to those in Christian service, with the permission of *The Baptist Bulletin*, I am reprinting "Christian Friction," by Wally Stephenson. These principles apply to every believer in Jesus Christ.

An administrator of a large mission reported, "Ninety-five percent of problems on the mission field and in churches involve interpersonal relationships." The speaker is not given to exaggeration and has forty-five years of experience both as an active missionary and as a mission administrator. I was shocked. My initial reaction was sadness. How tragic that Christians cannot get along with one another, causing broken relationships, divisions, injury, and defamation to the cause of Christ. Valuable time, money, and opportunities are wasted because believers won't settle their differences. Yet, the Bible gives basic principles to guide our relationships with other Christians.

Principle One: Reconcile First

In the Sermon on the Mount, Jesus teaches, *"Therefore if you bring your gift to the altar, and there remember that your brother has something against you, leave your gift there before the altar, and go your way. First be reconciled to your brother, and then come and offer your gift"* (Matthew 5:23–24).

When I recognize a brother has something against me, I have a responsibility to go to him and try to resolve the problem. Other spiritual duties can wait.

Why don't we practice Matthew 5:23–24? One reason is pride. Another is unwillingness to humble ourselves. We fear we will have to admit we are wrong. We are more concerned about our image than about the name of Christ, the spiritual well-being of a Christian brother, and the Body of Christ.

Principle Two: Go to the Offender

Jesus outlined the steps a believer must follow when he has been offended. *"Moreover, if your brother sins against you, go and tell him his fault between you and him alone. If he hears you, you have gained your brother. But if he will not hear, take with you one or two more, that by the mouth of two or three witnesses every word may be established. And if he refuses to hear them, tell it to the church. But if he refuses even to hear the church, let him be to you like a heathen and a tax collector"* (Matthew 18:15–17).

At least two are involved in a dispute. One is the offended party, the other the person causing the offense. People typically expect the offender to approach them. Most times the offended person does not confront the one who offended him, as Jesus commanded. Instead, he tells everyone else his grievance. Other people shouldn't listen, but they do. As people take sides, the problem gets spread around the Christian community—embellished, yet tragically unresolved. Sometimes Christians air their "dirty laundry" before unbelievers, who respond inwardly—and often outwardly—by scoffing and belittling Christianity. What perverted thinking causes Christians to speak and act in such a way?

Principle Three: Accept Differences in "Gray" Areas

"Let not him who eats despise him who does not eat, and let not him who does not eat judge him who eats; for God has

received him" (Romans 14:3).

A "gray area" is a subject not specifically mentioned in the Bible, one on which Christians disagree. For example, I put music into categories: "great," "tolerable," "noise," and "sinful." I can accept a brother who listens to "tolerable" and "noise," and not make an issue of it, nor break fellowship over it. Each one stands accountable to God, not to me, for his listening, eating, exercising, and other practices. Who am I to judge God's servant if he doesn't dot his "i's" and cross his "t's" exactly as I do?

Principle Four: Create No Stumbling Blocks

"Therefore let us not therefore judge one another anymore, but rather resolve this, not to put a stumbling block or a cause to fall in our brother's way" (Romans 14:13).

At a wedding reception, my wife, Louise, and I sat with a couple we had never met. When drinks were served, we declined the alcohol. At the end of the evening the couple said, "Recently we became born-again Christians, and we prayed that God would show us whether we should drink or not." If a weaker brother copied my action and example, would it predispose him to sin? I *am* my brother's keeper. I have a responsibility not to offend his convictions, cause him to fall into sin, or lead him astray.

Principle Five: Build Up One Another

"Let each of us please his neighbour for his good, leading to edification" (Romans 15:2). *"Let no corrupt word proceed out of your mouth, but what is good for necessary edification, that it may impart grace unto the hearers"* (Ephesians 4:29).

It is so easy to get sidetracked from this principle because human beings naturally do things that meet their own needs and bring pleasure to themselves. It is difficult to consistently love and build up others with all their idiosyncrasies, but believers have been given a new nature and have the Holy Spirit to enable them to do exactly that.

Principle Six: Settle Matters Quickly

"But, speaking the truth in love . . . putting away lying, let each one of you speak truth with his neighbor, for we are members of one another. Be angry and do not sin; do not let the sun go down on your wrath, nor give place to the devil" (Ephesians 4:15 and 25–27).

Some believers speak the truth, not in love, but in a harsh, condemning way. This is wrong. If someone makes us angry, we are commanded to settle the dispute as soon as possible. Satan loves to see differences drag on because that gives him more time to wreak havoc.

Principle Seven: Forgive, and Forgive, and Forgive

"Be kind to one another, even as God in Christ forgave you" (Ephesians 4:32).

Peter asked Jesus in Matthew 18:21, *"How often shall . . . I forgive him?"* Peter suggested seven as a generous number, but Jesus answered, *"seventy times seven"* (490), by which I believe He meant an infinite number.

Why do Christians get on each other's nerves, in each other's hair, and at each other's throats? James 4:1–3 teaches that evil desires, wrong motives, and pride are root causes of conflict. Our gracious Father has given us a new nature, His indwelling Holy Spirit, and the teachings of His Word to help us live harmoniously with one another. What more do we need? The answer is a believer's loving, submissive, wholehearted obedience.

—*The Baptist Bulletin*, March 2000

BETWEEN THE LINES

Specifically for Cross-cultural Missionaries

In his book *Facing the Field*, Dr. Stanley Soltau counsels:

It often happens that two or more families or individuals are thrown together in the same mission station who, from the standpoint of temperament or culture, seem to have very little in common. Had they lived in the same town at home, they would, in all probability, never have formed a friendship that was in any sense close. On the mission field, however, they may be the only Westerners in the city and are entirely dependent upon each other for their spiritual fellowship and social life. Grace will often be required to keep relations between them sweet, but the giver of all grace is able to grant it in sufficient quantity so as to insure victory.

On the other hand when two or more families or individuals are compatible, the combined impact of their work and influence is cumulative. The moral and spiritual discipline which they undergo as they work together, checking and counterchecking on each other's efforts, precludes the tendency toward becoming dictatorial and difficult. In the long run they will accomplish much more, both quantitatively and qualitatively, than had they been placed singly and alone in different places."[1]

Distance, isolation, loneliness, pressure of surrounding non-Christian religions, and the necessities of the common work all unite to force cross-cultural missionaries into closer circumstances than is true of Christian workers elsewhere. In such circumstances small annoyances that under other conditions might go unnoticed, are apt to be magnified and develop into serious irritations.

A missionary doctor said of an ongoing conflict, "If I have to

build them with my own hands, I am going to get each of these single women into a house of her own. Their constant squabbling is driving us all crazy." If justified, what a terrible indictment!
Learn to live peaceably, as we read in Romans 2:18.

 To those who are unmarried: As an unmarried person you may be assigned to live with someone you would not have chosen to have a cup of coffee or a coke with at home. You have nothing in common. Maybe your housemate is old enough to be your mother. Or, in this era of "Finishers" you—as a mature person with one or more careers behind you—might find your "senior missionary" barely more than a giggling teenager—at least in your eyes. Still the decree stands: "Learn to live peaceably." God knew it would be a learning process.

Women living in the same house need time to work out their day-by-day arrangements. It takes as much time and effort learning to adjust to this type of living situation as it does when you are married. In fact, one widow, serving in a short-term missionary capacity remarked, "I didn't have half the trouble cooking for my husband as I do for the women in my house."

A harmonious living situation doesn't "just happen." It takes work, as well as trial and error. Here are three suggestions that have helped in various situations:

1. As you organize your household schedule, set aside time to pray together.
2. Keep short accounts with one another.
3. Get a touchy matter straightened out as soon as possible.

I am grateful for the first roommates I had as a new missionary. Becky Davey and I moved in with Juanita Canfield, who had arrived a few years before we did and, therefore, was our senior missionary. She often regimented us and bossed us about (all for our ultimate welfare, as we admitted later on). But sometimes I rebelled at her telling me what to do. I remember one stormy breakfast when we were at loggerheads. Juanita left to tutor a language class of new missionaries, and I stayed to take care of their kids. She had been gone barely a few minutes when she returned. "I couldn't leave it like that," she said. A reconciliation, a brief prayer—and we both were free to enjoy the day before us. Don't harbor resentments or allow bitterness to grow between you and those with whom you live. Here are some other considerations:

- Be careful in your honest search for harmony in your home that you don't lose your own identity. Don't live in each other's pockets. Be a person in your own right.

- Don't be a leech, always clinging to your housemate or to one particular friend. Circumstances change so fast. Enjoy the situation you are in but allow for the possibility of a change in location, job, or marital status in the future.

- When two men or two women share a house, be sure to get across to him or her and the rest of your associates that you are not conjoined twins. You don't have to do everything together. You don't have to be invited out together. You don't have to take vacations together. It's better if you have separate interests that you can talk about later when you are together. Learn to say "no" to an invitation that you can't fit into your schedule or if you don't feel like going. But do this with sensitivity. Your "no" may deprive your housemate of something he or she wishes to attend.

A word of caution, even as we are talking about creating an attitude of kindness and concern. Some beautiful friendships have developed between women who live in the same house and work, laugh, and cry together. Be especially careful, however, that the relationship does not develop along physical lines. As St. Augustine described it so long ago. "Some pollute the stream of friendship with the sludge of unbridled sex." His statement applies equally to single men and married couples as well as single women.

To those who are married: In the area of daily living, married couples have the advantage of having chosen each other rather than being placed with a housemate. They already know each other's shortcomings and faults—at least the ones that surface in a relatively stable environment and temperate climate. They have love to buffer the bad spots in life. But even in the best of marriages, problems develop with the stresses of a new culture, new responsibilities, different food, and extreme weather conditions.

Married couples need to plan times when they can be alone together. *A word to the unmarried:* don't feel you always have to be part of every group. Give the couples space to enjoy themselves. You might offer to babysit so that they can have time alone.

As was previously suggested for the singles living in close quarters, the marrieds, too, need to keep short accounts with one another and with God. Don't let resentments build up until they are irreconcilable.

Sometimes just the differences in personality—that which makes a person uniquely who he or she is—can be the very thing that causes friction.

- One might be sociable, always wanting to have guests and be on the go.
- The other might be more reserved and would much rather stay at home.
- One might be a perfectionist, a stickler for neatness.
- The other might like the house to have a lived-in look.

THE CHALLENGE OF PEACEFUL LIVING

Whether talking of housemates or marriage partners, recognizing basic differences in temperament can be a great plus. *Spirit Controlled Temperament*, by Tim LaHaye, examines four basic temperaments: sanguine, choleric, melancholy, and phlegmatic. He explains that all temperaments have their strengths and weaknesses, but in Christ there is strength for every weakness. If you have never read this book, or haven't read it for a while, go through it again.

Some organizations require members to take the DISC Personality Style Survey. DISC® is the original, oldest, most validated, reliable, personal assessment used by millions to improve lives, interpersonal relationships, work productivity, teamwork, and communication. The initials stand for **D**ominance, **I**nfluence, **S**teadiness, and **C**onscientiousness. Visit www.discprofile.com to learn more.

While you may not subscribe to these philosophies, it helps when you understand that generally people act the way they do because they were made that way. They are not deliberately trying to annoy you!

BETWEEN THE LINES

Personalities Differ

When Lynn and I first started sharing a home, I often distressed her unwittingly. Coming in from a lesson or a medical call, I dropped whatever I had been using on the nearest table and let the stuff lie there until I had time for a grand-slam clean up. Lynn, on the other hand, put things where they belonged immediately, working on the probability that the great clean-up might not happen right away. I certainly didn't mean to annoy her; leaving things in plain sight was an incentive for me to get going on the tidy-up job. Looking back, I realize I always enjoyed doing things in a big way. During those Saturday morning clean-ups in my parsonage

homes, many times I pulled everything out of the drawers and
cupboards to be resorted and organized, rather than dusting and
running the vacuum cleaner.

Traits and lifelong habits are not easy to break. Be considerate
with your co-workers. Each of us has quirks of personality that are
irritating or even offensive to others.

If the actions or characteristics of a person with whom you live
or work drive you crazy, ask yourself, "Is what he or she is doing
adversely affecting the Lord's work, or is it just something that
bothers me personally?" If the latter is true, it could be that praying for that person will change your attitude entirely.

An even more penetrating question to ask yourself is, "What
am *I* doing that is driving someone crazy? Do people have to spend
time praying for grace to put up with me?"

A mark of maturity is working on eliminating your own quirks
and accepting those of others. Rather than deciding that your colleague is out to rub salt in your wound, learn and practice the
advice of Jonathan Goforth, missionary to China. In 1894 he com-
piled seven rules for daily living. Among them is: "Put the very
best construction on the actions of others."

Don't ascribe underlying or ulterior motives to a person's
actions. Assume he is doing what he thinks is best. God has not set
you or me up as judge over our fellow-workers.

Two quotations are applicable here. The first is by Kipling: "Be
slow to judge. We know little of what has been done, and nothing
of what has been resisted."

The other is a First Nations adage. "Do not judge a man until
you have walked a mile in his moccasins."

Be careful in handing out criticisms, whether they are of a person, or his family, or his work. When a reprimand or suggestion needs to be given, remember the formula, *"speaking the truth in love"* (Ephesians 4:15a).

As much as you try to live without ruffling anybody's feathers, problems are bound to arise. The close confines within which many Christian workers live and work can be a hothouse, producing friction and trouble.

Healthy conflict, however, is not necessarily a bad thing. It can help a team work through issues and move ahead in ministry instead of always taking the easy, non-turbulent path. Some people do not want the boat ever to be rocked, and they miss opportunities to make the team stronger and better.

TELL IT LIKE IT IS

Often, when a missionary speaks at missions' conferences or to women's groups, an attendee looks intensely at the speakers and says: "We want to know what it is really like to be a missionary. Tell us about daily life with other Christian workers." The missionaries glance at one another with that "Do they really want to know?" look.

Listen in on a church ladies' meeting where missionary women from different countries answer. One missionary is single; one is newly married; the third is married with several children:

Single missionary: I walk a fine line, trying not to offend my married colleagues. I feel like I do everything. I'm always involved, always giving myself. But then my co-worker's wife complains that I haven't made an effort to spend time with her going shopping or doing other "girly" things.

Married with children: I wish somebody would acknowledge that I'm actually busy, too. Between language study, helping my husband's ministry, and rearing three kids, I barely have time to take a shower, much less get involved in every ministry there is. Single women have more time; they should do more. But I'm so tired of them comparing their level of ministry activity to mine and judging me to be inferior.

Newly married: I started out as a single missionary and really liked it, even though sometimes I felt as if I was treated like one of the missionary kids. When I got married, my single missionary friends still expected me to have them over and get together for fun things as often as I used to. It's not that I don't want to, but dealing with several health issues, my recent marriage, and culture shock, I just don't feel I have anything left. They think I've become a snob. I wish they'd try to understand.

Single: Understand? I wish someone would try to understand me! Married women have husbands to bounce things off, talk things through with. I live alone and I give so much of myself to the work. Don't I deserve to hang out with Western friends sometimes?

Married with children: Sure, but if you're lonely, it's not the married women's fault. I should be allowed to focus my time on the nationals and my family without being expected to host a lot of parties to make life easier for the singles.

Newly married: I feel as if I'm not accepted in either camp. Since I'm married, the singles don't connect with me anymore; but since I don't have kids, I don't fit in with the families either. Can't I belong even though I'm in a separate category?

Single: "Separate"—yes, that's the right word for me. Married people just don't get it. I have to clean my own car, fix my own sink, and pay my own bills. And still I get the feedback—very unexpected from a married colleague—that when I am with her and her husband, I talk only to him and, therefore, obviously think I am superior to her. What? I think of them as a unit. And how does she reach the conclusion that I think I am superior? Can't we just celebrate each other without judging?

Married with children: That would be nice, but do you really believe you're a victim here? That you're not doing any judging yourself? There are thousands of women in North America who are single, many who have children. They work full time and have to raise kids while doing all those things you're complaining about. Seems you feel you've got it harder than anybody else.

Single: You can say that because the others on the team don't expect much from you. You get to stay home and play with your kids and have mothers' Bible studies that we are left out of. We are expected to be full time in the ministry and ignore not just the teasing of our male colleagues but even being treated like lesser beings by the nationals because we're just women and our fathers "couldn't find us husbands."

Married with children: Do you think I wouldn't love to be out there more? Do you know how hard it was to give up my identity as a missionary and now be looked at as "just" a wife and mother? The Bible says it's a significant calling, but it sure is hard to believe that when everybody treats you as if you're just staying home painting your nails! And then there's my single teammate who thinks I'm not keeping my home properly, telling me what my husband's favorite dishes are and catering to him when she's at my home. I'm sick of . . . and I wish . . .

By this time, the church women were in stunned silence, eyebrows high, mouths agape, and thinking: *Aren't these missionary women supposed to be spiritual giants? Aren't they supposed to love God, to care about the national workers and each other more than themselves?*

Some who read the preceding made-up dialogue may see it as a lot of complaining, a bunch of sour grapes. Actually, each of the situations has happened to some woman missionary at some time. Circumstances differ, of course, according to the size and make-up of the team of co-workers and how closely they live and work together.

The painful fact is that God uses ordinary people, sinners saved by grace to do His work. Missionary women (and men) don't always feel or act as they should. Some missionaries have been genuinely mistreated; some missionaries have done the mistreating. Misunder-standings, making assumptions, and passing judgments can quickly escalate if not dealt with in a godly and loving way.

Living peaceably is not easy. Each of us is selfish by nature. We think our way is the only way, or at least the best way. We must consistently work at living in peace and harmony.

What Can You Do When Problems Arise?

Two words come to mind: compromise and flexibility.

- Compromise—a settlement of differences by which each side makes concessions
- Flexibility—able to adjust and change

These attitudes open the door for give-and-take on both sides. No one is ever either completely right or completely wrong; both can give a bit.

One year, three nurse colleagues and a Peace Corps nurse vacationed together in India. Since none of us had money for hotels, we stayed at missionary quarters. One night we stayed with two women, one of whom had served in India for decades. The other—like us—was a newcomer. The older woman had carefully tutored the man who served the table to bring first the meat, then the gravy, and then the potatoes. The younger missionary wanted to put the gravy on her potatoes. The two women fussed over this every evening. They barely spoke to one another; they certainly couldn't pray together. For the Peace Corps nurse, this was her first introduction to missionaries. She was wide-eyed over the gravy issue. One of us innocently suggested, "Why don't you just put the gravy on the table? That way you could have it whenever you want it." They hadn't thought of that solution!

Sometimes "live peaceably" comes down to the most basic areas of living. When Wally and I go grocery shopping, I have my trusty list and check off items as I find them. Not Wally. He searches out bargains, some of which we don't need and have no room to store. I usually give him free rein and smile as he loads his finds into the cart. And I remember a scene in a Giant Supermarket in New Cumberland, Pennsylvania.

A couple came in to shop, obviously harried after a busy day at work. The wife was snatching items off shelves in her rush to get home. Along came her husband proudly carrying two roasts of beef, "Look, Honey, TWO for the price of one." She snapped, "Put those things back. We don't even need one." He trotted back to the meat department like a puppy with its tail between its legs. I never want to see on Wally's face the look that was in that man's eyes.

PRIVACY

In addition to differences in personality, another irritant is the failure to respect other people's privacy.

Privacy is essentially a Western value. North Americans, especially, derive a sense of security from privacy. They have their own bedrooms, closets, dresser drawers, and perhaps locked files or diaries. They resent people peering at them, prying into their business, or giving unsolicited advice.

To the Asian mind—and certainly in Bangladesh—privacy is practically incomprehensible. Eastern people derive security from togetherness. In many lower-class homes, the entire family lives in one room. If a person is ill, everyone flocks to visit, to commiserate, and to reinterpret the doctor's orders. When a new bride goes to her husband's home, her younger sister may go along to make sure the bride won't be lonely.

Decisions are not private matters. They are made in mutual consultation among the older, most respected members of the community, then passed down to the younger ones, who rarely question or disobey. Decisions as to whom one will marry, where one will study or live, what name to give a new baby: These are all made by the group, possibly without even much consideration of the feelings of the people most closely involved. Everyone is very much his brother's keeper and will offer free advice or interfere in a situation in order to protect what he thinks is in another person's best interests. Often a person will be swayed from heading off in a wrong direction in life, or, sadly, from accepting Christ as Savior, by the expedient of reminding him of his obligation to the group to which he belongs. "Who do you think you are, doing something that none of the rest of us has ever done?" And the matter is dropped.

As part of the two worlds in which the missionary lives, he must be like a chameleon, changing his outlook as the situation demands. When local people want to see your house—show them. When they ask questions, answer them—within reason, of course. But when you return to your peer group, return privacy to its priority place on the Western value scale. This includes things such as:

- Never walk into someone's house or room without first knocking on the door or calling out, "Anybody home?" or in some other way announcing yourself.
- Never burst in on a conversation.
- Never read another person's mail, whether by shuffling through his desk or steaming open the envelopes. (Besides being totally impolite, it could be humiliating: You might find out something about yourself you'd be happier not knowing.)
- Never help yourself to somebody's clothes or car or computer without prior permission. And periodically check your bookshelves to be sure you have not inadvertently become a "book-keeper."

Going deeper than respecting a person's belongings is respecting the person himself. Allow people to be individuals; let various families do things differently. Your family has its own identity. The children need to learn: "We're the Jones family. We do things this way. At the Smiths' house, they do it another way."

BLESSED ARE THE PEACEMAKERS

We have discussed a few ingredients that make for peaceable relationships. One reason this is so important is the special emphasis the Lord Himself gives. In Matthew 5:9, *"Blessed are the peacemakers, for they shall be called the sons of God."*

Periodically, we need to reflect on the question: Are human relationships smoother and more loving where I am, or do problems needlessly arise and petty contentions grow because of me?

One of our chief desires, as people called to serve the Lord, ought to be to create an atmosphere of harmony, love, and care for one another. It ought to be that outsiders coming to our homes, our offices, and our classrooms can see the love of Christ radiating through our daily living. Only then will our witness be credible as we endeavor to attract people to Christ. They will see Him in us—in the way we act and the way we treat our fellow workers—and will be drawn to know more about Him. Or, they will see in us bitterness, jealousies, and pettiness, and they will turn away from Him.

Our dealings with one another transcend the artificial boxes labeled Singles, Married, New Worker, or Veteran. It is how we treat each other as people, as fellow members of the family of God, that really counts.

Lord, make me an instrument of Your peace.
Where there is hatred, let me show LOVE;
Where there is injury, PARDON;
Where there is discord, UNITY;
Where there is doubt, FAITH;
Where there is error, TRUTH;
Where there is despair, HOPE;
Where there is sadness, JOY;
Where there is darkness, LIGHT.

—St. Francis of Assisi

---

[1] Stanley Soltau, *Facing the Field* (Grand Rapids, Baker Book House, 1975), 86–88.

LIFE'S LESSONS I'M TRYING TO LEARN

SUGGESTIONS FOR THE JOURNEY

Having read through this book, you realize I have been on life's journey for quite a while. The longer I live and the farther I travel, the more I realize the importance of Paul's words in 1 Corinthians 13:13. Speaking of the trio of faith, hope, and love, he wrote, *"The greatest of these is LOVE."* May I make these suggestions:

• Love the Lord your God with all your heart and soul and mind.
• Love your own family dearly.
• Love your co-workers.
• Love the people among whom you live and work.

For those just starting the adventure of serving
  the Lord,
I envy you and say, "Enjoy the journey."

For those in the middle years where the doldrums
  sometimes hit,
I say, "Hang in there," and

For those nearing the end, to you
I say, "Finish well."

"Now to Him who is able to keep you from stumbling, and to present you faultless before the presence of his glory with exceeding joy. To God, our Savior, who alone is wise, be glory and majesty, dominion and power, both now and forever. Amen" (Jude, verse 24).

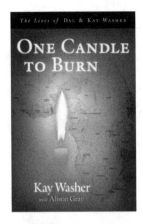

One Candle to Burn
by Kay Washer

Dallas and Kay Washer shared Christ's love in Africa by preaching to jungle tribes, rescuing unwanted babies, founding a ministry for blind children, and helping to start a hospital. Along the way, they loved and laughed and built a family that, between all family members, has now served over a hundred years in Africa and continues to serve there today.

Interwoven
by Russ & Nancy Ebersole

Four years after the deaths of their mates, God led Russ and Nancy together and blended their families. *Interwoven* describes the many threads God wove together and recounts unusual situations they have experienced, such as a hijacking to communist China.

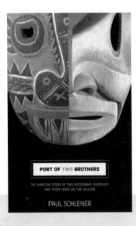

Port of Two Brothers
by Paul Schlener

The astonishing story of how God led and used brothers Paul & John Schlener to draw hundreds of indigenous people in an Amazon village to Himself.

Kubanka Kids
by Donna Messenger

Five stories, each with four full-page illustrations, based on lives of actual children and ABWE's work with them in Kubanka, Ukraine. Provides an unforgettable glimpse into the lives of Ukrainian children and the need for missionaries there. CD for picture projection included.

NEW!
A 5-DAY MISSIONS RESOURCE!

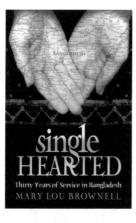

Singlehearted
by Mary Lou Brownell

Mary Lou Brownell served as a missionary in Bangladesh for thirty years, nursing in jungle clinics, directing nursing at the ABWE mission hospital, establishing a training center for destitute women widowed by the war, and sharing the gospel at every opportunity.

In the Air for Him
by Ruth Scheltema

Ruth and Hank Scheltema's pioneering aviation ministry in the Amazon and the beginning of ABWE Air.

HOW TO ORDER

Write to:
ABWE Publishing
P.O. Box 8585
Harrisburg, PA 17105

Toll-free:
1-877-959-ABWE (2293)
publish@abwe.org
www.abwe.org